Kid's Box

Updated Second Edition

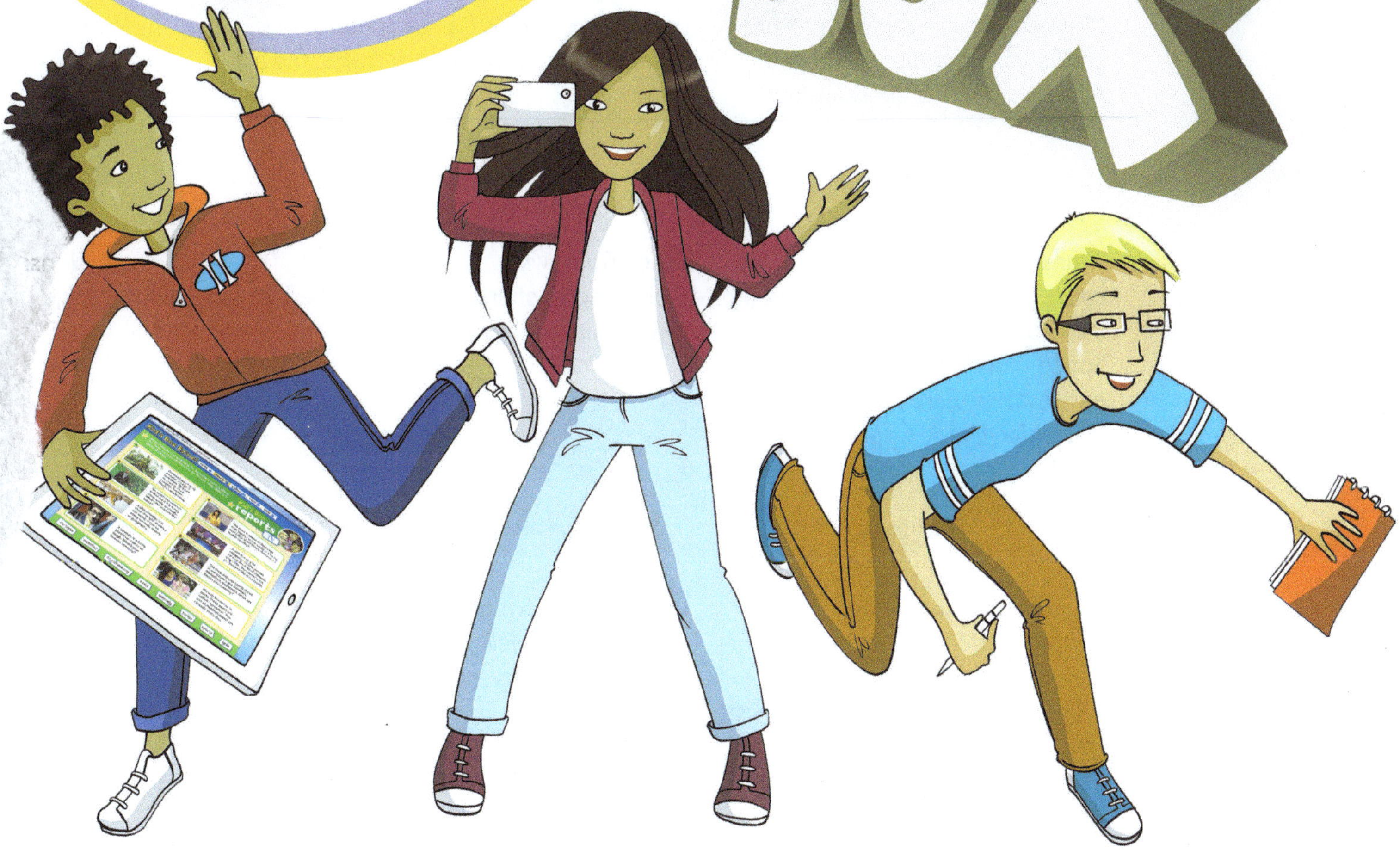

Student's Book 6
American English

Caroline Nixon & Michael Tomlinson

Language summary

	Key vocabulary	Key grammar and functions	Phonics
High technology — page 4	Technology: app, cell phone, chat, electronic whiteboard, email, ezine, flash drive, headphones, Internet, keyboard, laptop, microphone, mouse, MP3, screen, speakers, text message, webcam Schoolwork: article, competition, project, win adjectives	Review of present tenses and their uses Questions: Do you have … ? Do you … ? Can you … ?	Compound nouns
1 Beastly tales — page 10	Theater: act, actor, audition, part (in a play), play (n) Myths and legends: beast, breathe, claws, eagle, feathers, fur, hero, horn, legend, myth, nest, scales Mythical beasts: centaur, dragon, griffin, harpy (harpies), mermaid, Minotaur, phoenix, siren, unicorn	Plans, intentions, and predictions: going to Describing creatures: It has the body of a lizard, They have feathers, They live in nests Joining clauses with who, where, that: Icarus, the boy <u>who</u> flew too close to the Sun. The nests <u>where</u> griffins live are made of gold. A dragon is a beast <u>that</u> has scales and big claws.	Consonant sounds: voiced and unvoiced "th" (w<u>e</u>a<u>th</u>er, <u>th</u>eater)

Art · Myths and legends   page 16

	Key vocabulary	Key grammar and functions	Phonics
2 Tomorrow's world — page 18	Transport: carry (passengers), catch, get lost, pick up, transport (n), travel by (air/bus, etc.) Space travel: air, astronaut, businessman, Earth, engineer, flight, float, Moon, rocket, space, tourist, weigh	Predictions: will Connectors: after that, because, before, then, when	Contractions: 'll, 'm, 're, 's, n't

Science · The solar system   page 24   Review 1 and 2   page 26

	Key vocabulary	Key grammar and functions	Phonics
3 The great outdoors — page 28	The country: adventure, break (an arm / a leg), cave, fall over, hole, rock, waterfall, woods (place) Compass points: north, south, east, west Exploration: backpack, camp (v), come back, expedition, explorer, flashlight, journey, land (n), leave (v), sled, sleeping bag, tent	Past progressive and simple past: I was climbing when I fell. Describing location: Oldbridge is east of the mountains.	Consonant sounds: "k" (<u>c</u>oat, ki<u>ck</u>) and "g" (<u>g</u>oat, bi<u>g</u>)

Art · Landscape painting   page 34

		Key vocabulary	Key grammar and functions	Phonics
4	Food, glorious food! page 36	Food: butter, candy, chopsticks, cookie, coffee, dish (part of a meal), fruit, hot dog, jelly, pan, peanuts, peas, popcorn, recipe, sauce, snack, strawberry, sushi, vegetables	Count and non-count nouns: We don't have enough eggs. We have too many apples. We have too much sugar.	Pronouncing the letters "gh": night, laugh, cough
	Science — Micro-organisms page 42		Review 3 and 4 page 44	
5	Under the ocean page 46	Seas and oceans: claw, coral, crab, jellyfish, lobster, mammal, octopus, reef, rescue, seal, shell, squid, turtle	Present perfect with for, since, still: The whale's been here for three hours. I've lived here since 2008. We still haven't chosen a project.	Stressed syllables: bottle, today
	Science — Food chains page 52			
6	Free time page 54	Free time and hobbies: beatbox, bike trail, board game, chess, fashion design, do tricks, drum, free running, jigsaw puzzle, mountain bike, play an instrument, sew, skateboard	Quantifiers: some, any, no, every, someone, anyone, no one, everyone, something, anything, nothing, everything, somewhere, anywhere, nowhere, everywhere	Short vowel sound: "u" (fun, cousin, London)
	Music — Popular music page 60		Review 5 and 6 page 62	
7	Dress sense page 64	Clothes: belt, button, coat, decorate, fashion, gloves, jacket, nylon, pocket, protect, shorts, stockings, umbrella Adjectives: heavy, light, thick, thin	Possibility: may, might Describing clothes: He's wearing gray pants. Describing pictures: There are some people outside a movie theater. I can see …	Intonation for expressing feelings
	History — Clothes page 70			
8	Around the world page 72	Countries and nationalities: Brazil, Brazilian, France, French, Germany, German, Greece, Greek, India, Indian, Mexico, Mexican, Portugal, Portuguese, Spain, Spanish	Present perfect with just, yet, already Regular and irregular past participles	Intonation in lists

Language — The history of words page 78   Review 7 and 8 page 80

Values 1 & 2 — Living with technology page 82   Values 3 & 4 — Be safe at home page 83

Values 5 & 6 — Harmony at home page 84   Values 7 & 8 — Sharing problems page 85

Grammar reference page 86   Flyers practice test page 88

High technology

🔦 **Show what you know!** What technology words can you remember?

Listening 1 🎧 02 CD1 Listen and check (✓) the technology words you hear.

2 🎧 03 CD1 Listen again. Who said it?

1 Hi, Maria. How are you? **Dan.**
2 It's twenty-five after ten.
3 I have a text message on my cell.
4 There's a new ezine competition on the Internet.
5 Let's write something for it.
6 Why don't we do our first ezine article on technology?

3 Read and choose the right words.

1 Alex **doesn't** / **don't** arrive early.
2 Why **has** / **is** Alex late?
3 The game **starting** / **starts** in five minutes.
4 Dan **is** / **has** a text message.
5 **There are** / **There is** a prize for the best school ezine.
6 The winners can **write** / **writing** for the international school ezine.
7 Why **don't** / **doesn't** we write about technology?
8 Maria thinks it **sound** / **sounds** exciting.

🔍 **LOOK**

The game **starts** in five minutes.
I **don't** know.
Where **is** he?
The winners **can write** for the international school ezine.

4 Read and answer.

1. What's an ezine?
2. Who can enter the competition?
3. How often must they write an article?
4. What should the article include?
5. How many computers can they win?
6. What kind of ezine do the winners write for?

Annual Internet Magazine Competition
Write an ezine project and help your school. It's open to all schools with students between the ages of 7 and 12. Students must write an ezine project every month. The article should be interesting and include text and pictures. There are two important prizes. The best ezine wins ten new computers for your school. The winners also write an article every month for the international school ezine.

5 Listen and check (✓) the box.

1. What's Alex using to write to his mom?

2. What are Dan and Maria playing?

3. What's Maria listening to?

4. What are Alex and Dan looking at?

6 Read and answer.

When we text on our cell phones, we don't use all the letters, so we can write more quickly. In a text we don't always put the vowels (a, e, i, o, u), and we choose letters or numbers that sound the same, for example U (you), R (are), C (see), 2 (to, too), and 4 (for). There are some short sentences, too. LOL (laugh out loud) means "It's really funny." We don't always use punctuation (capital letters, commas, question marks, and so on).

Look at the cell phones. Can you understand the messages? Answer the questions.

1. cn u rd this
2. HW LD R U
3. do u hv a cmptr
4. WHTS UR FVRT MSC

7 Write three text messages for your friends to answer.

Reading

8 Read and think. Which is the smallest thing in the pictures?

http://www.cambridge.org/elt/kidsbox/ezine

Kid's Box Ezine!

home | reports | games | world | email

Kid's Box reports — Technology

Technology is changing our lives a lot, so this is the topic of our first ezine.

We use technology every day when we communicate and when we study and play. When we talk to people, this is called communication. We can talk in person, on the phone, or through the computer. On the computer we can talk into a microphone. If we want to see the other person on the screen, we use a small camera, called a webcam. We listen through small headphones, or we use speakers.

A lot of people use laptops, too. These computers are small and light, so people can carry them to different places.
A laptop has a screen and a keyboard, and it opens like a notebook. The smallest laptops weigh less than one and a half kilograms, but some people prefer to carry information from their computer on a flash drive, which they can carry anywhere.

We can also write to people when we want to communicate with them. We can write emails or text on our phones using apps. Emails and texts are quicker than letters, but "chatting" is the quickest way to communicate on a computer because different people can write messages at the same time or talk with each other face-to-face.

laptop | flash drive | speakers | microphone | headphones | webcam | keyboard | chat

9 🔊 Listen. Repeat the word and say the letter.   ▶ 1 Speakers.   Speakers. That's "d."

10 Read again and correct the sentences.

1 On a computer we talk into a flash drive.
2 A small computer is called a lapbox.
3 We can use a computer to text.
4 Other people can't hear if we use speakers.
5 We can carry information on a microphone.
6 We can see people with a keyboard.

11 Read and complete.

> We use high technology
> ~~An electronic whiteboard on the wall~~
> Or just watch the TV
> The keyboard does it all
> We watch videos on the screen

We have flash drives in our school bags,

(1) **An electronic whiteboard on the wall**.

We have laptops,
Headphones, and MP3s.
Hear the future call!

Now we text on cell phones,
(2) _____.
We communicate by Internet
And watch movies on DVD.

We take pictures with our phones,
(3) _____.
We use programs for a dictionary
To find out what words mean.

Some just play computer games
(4) _____.
They don't use their imagination
Or think or speak or listen.

We don't need pens or paper —
(5) _____!
There are robots in our factories.
Hear the future call!

12 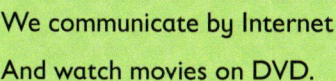 Listen and check. Sing the song.

13 Invent another verse.

14 Read and complete.

> screen   flash drive   speakers
> keyboard   emails   webcam
> ~~laptop~~   chat

This is my special Techno Box. It's the best (1) **laptop** in the world. It's small and light, and I can carry it in a special bag. When I open it, there's a (2) _____ for me to watch DVDs and read my (3) _____. It has a small (4) _____ on it, so my friends can see me when we (5) _____. I can carry my pens and pencils under the (6) _____, which I use to write. My (7) _____, which goes below the pencil sharpeners, can carry a lot of information, especially music and pictures. I can listen to my music through the (8) _____ or use my headphones.

15 Imagine another invention. Write about it.

16 Focus on phonics

He's at the **airport** with his **laptop**,

She's buying **postcards** at the **bookstore**,

He has a **toothbrush** in his **suitcase**,

She got an **armchair** for her **birthday**!

Speaking **17** Make questions. Ask and answer.

> Do you have a cell phone?   Do you sometimes chat online?

Find someone who ...	Name
1 has a cell phone	Ignacio
2 sometimes chats online	Marina
3 has a computer game	
4 can use an app on their phone or tablet	
5 listens to music on an MP3 player	
6 _____	
7 _____	

Writing **18** Write a report.

I spoke to ten people about technology. Only three of them have ... , but all of them can ...

 Joke Corner

Which mouse doesn't eat cheese?

A computer mouse!

1 Beastly tales

Show what you know! What animals can you remember?

Listening 1 🎧 Listen and check (✓) the animals you hear.

2 🎧 Listen again and answer the questions.

1 What time's the audition going to be? — A quarter to four.
2 Who's going to go to the audition?
3 Which part's he going to do?
4 Who's going to be King of the Beasts?
5 Which part are they going to give Dan?
6 What are they going to write about?

3 Read and match.

1 Who's going to
2 The audition
3 Dan's going to
4 Maria and Alex are
5 Dan isn't going to
6 Maria and Alex aren't going
7 What are they going

a is going to be on Wednesday.
b to be in the play.
c go to the audition.
d be the monkey.
e to write about?
f be in the play?
g going to watch him.

LOOK
I'm **going to go** to the audition.
We aren't **going to choose** you.
Are you **going to be** in the play?

4 Choose words from the box to complete the text.

| have | movies | want | bird | restaurant | see | rocks | ~~going~~ | pets | island |

Helen and Robert are (1) _going_ to go to the (2) _____ tomorrow. They're going to (3) _____ a movie called *My Family and Other Animals*. The movie's from a book by Gerald Durrell, and it's about his life when he was ten years old. In the movie the boy lives on an (4) _____. He has some friends, but a lot of his friends are different (5) _____. He has a (6) _____ called Ulysses, a turtle called Achilles, and a lot of spiders. Helen and Robert are going to have a great time because it's a very funny movie.

5 Read again and answer.
1 Where are Helen and Robert going to go?
2 What are they going to see?
3 What's the movie about?
4 How old is Gerald in the book?
5 What pets does Gerald have?
6 Why are Helen and Robert going to enjoy the movie?

6 Read and cross out the extra word.
1 We're are going to go to the theater tomorrow.
2 We aren't going to see at *The Lion King*.
3 I'm going to visit to my grandmother on Sunday.
4 What are you to going to see?
5 Where do are you going to sit?
6 She isn't going to sing on tonight.

7 Write questions with "going to."
1 Who / see / weekend?   Who are you going to see on the weekend?
2 What / do / Monday / after school?
3 play basketball / tomorrow afternoon?
4 Where / go / Friday / after school?
5 What / watch / TV / tomorrow?
6 When / do / homework?

8 Ask and answer.

(Who are you going to see on the weekend?)   (I'm going to see my cousins.)

Reading

9 Read and think. How many of the beasts are part bird?

http://www.cambridge.org/elt/kidsbox/ezine

Kid's Box Ezine!

home | reports | games | world | email

Kid's Box reports — Myths

There are many ancient stories from different countries. Some are about heroes and strange and exciting beasts that aren't real. These stories are called myths.

a  Griffins have the head, wings, front legs, and claws of an eagle and the body and back legs of a lion. They make nests from gold.

b A dragon is a beast that has the body of a lizard, so they don't have fur like a cat or feathers like a bird; they have scales like a fish. Some dragons have a bat's wings, and some can breathe fire.

c A unicorn is a beautiful white horse with one long horn on its head. It has a goat's feet and beard and a lion's tail.

d The centaur is part horse, too, but it has a man's head and top half of the body and the body and legs of a horse.

e  Sirens and harpies are part bird, part woman, but they're different. Sirens live close to water. They sing beautifully, but they're dangerous because they cause people to sail their boats onto rocks.

f Harpies are uglier than sirens. They live in nests and steal food from people.

g Sometimes people think sirens are the same as mermaids, but mermaids are half woman, half fish. They have beautiful long hair, but they don't have legs. They have a big fish tail with scales.

eagle | claws | horn | feathers | scales | dragon | nest | mermaid

10 Listen. Repeat the word and say the letters. ▶ 1 Claws. — Claws. That's "a" and "f."

11 Read again and say "yes" or "no."
1 Griffins have feathers on their wings.
2 A dragon has the body of a lizard.
3 A unicorn has two horns.
4 A centaur has a goat's beard.
5 Harpies live in nests.
6 Sirens and mermaids are the same.

12 Listen and choose the right words.
1 The story about the phoenix is a **song** / **myth** / **game**.
2 The phoenix was a beautiful **bird** / **lion** / **horse**.
3 The phoenix lived for **five** / **fifty** / **five hundred** years.
4 The first people to believe in the phoenix were the **Egyptians** / **Romans** / **Greeks**.
5 The phoenix was born in **a pond** / **a fire** / **a tree**.

13 Read and complete. Order the pictures.

| island | sings | ~~told~~ | Fleece | horse | sea |
| Greece | clearer | do | sports | song | |

Myths and legends, stories of old,
Beastly tales that people (1) _told_ ,
Adventures and monsters, strange animals, too,
Heroes who had great things to (2) _____ .

The Greeks are famous, not just for (3) _____ ,
But also for Jason and the Argonauts.
They wrote, in their mythology,
Of his adventures across the (4) _____ .

Jason's bad uncle made him look for the "fleece."
Special wool made of gold, so they tell us in (5) _____ .
He had a smart teacher, like yours, of course!
His teacher was a centaur – half man, half (6) _____ .

The teacher told him all about the dangerous siren
Who could break his boat on rocks around the (7) _____ .
She's half woman, half bird, with feathers and wings.
She sounds really beautiful when she (8) _____ .

The Argonauts were sailing, and before too long,
They started to hear the siren's (9) _____ .
It sounded beautiful, but they didn't go closer
"Cos Orpheus" music was louder and (10) _____ .

This is part of the myth from ancient Greece
Of Jason and the Golden (11) _____ .

14 Listen and check. Say the rap.

15 Invent an amazing mythical beast. Answer the questions.
1 What are you going to call it?
   I'm going to call it a ...
2 What's your beast going to look like?
   It's going to have a ...'s head, ...
3 What color's it going to be?
4 Is it going to have feathers, fur, or scales?
5 Does it have spots or stripes? What else is it going to have on its body?

16 Ask and answer about your beast in pairs.

17 Draw and write about your beast.

18 **Focus on phonics**

Th is is my my th ical creature;
Wi th a big mou th and golden fea th ers.
He loves acting in the th eater,
And swimming in sunny wea th er.

Speaking **19** Ask and answer. Use your imagination or the ideas in the box. Write your friend's answers.

> search for a dragon   explore an island   fly with a harpy
> sing with a siren   buy a pet griffin   swim with a mermaid
> play volleyball with a unicorn   sail across an ocean

What are you going to do next Monday?

I'm going to meet a centaur.

Monday	David's going to meet a centaur.
Tuesday	
Wednesday	
Thursday	
Friday	

Writing **20** Write an email about your plans.

Hi, Elena
Next week, I'm going to be very busy. On Monday I'm going to sail across an ocean with the Argonauts, and then …

Joke Corner

What kind of phone does a mermaid use?

A shell phone.

DIGGORY BONES

Art — Myths and legends

FACT: The characters in legends were often real people. King Arthur was a real person, but the sword in the stone is a legend.

1 Read and talk with your friend.

When we read books or someone tells us something, the information can be fact or fiction.

Fact means something that we know happened, is real, or is true.

Fiction means something that isn't real. It is imaginary.

Think of three kinds of fiction texts and three kinds of fact texts.

Myths and legends were some of the first stories that people told. Both of them are kinds of fiction. In Greek myths there is usually a hero, beasts, a quest with challenges (difficult things the hero must do), and someone who helps the hero.

Do you know any myths or legends? Talk about them. Who is in them? What do they do?

2 Read the story. Copy and complete the diagram.

Jason and the Argonauts

Jason was the son of a Greek king. His uncle, Pelias, was very bad and killed Jason's father because he wanted to become king. To protect Jason, his mother sent him to live with a centaur.

When he was older, Jason wanted to be king. Pelias wasn't happy, so he sent him on a very dangerous quest. He had to get the Golden Fleece and take it back to Pelias. This was difficult to get because a frightening dragon took care of it.

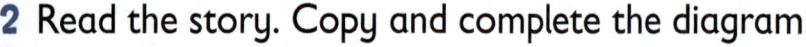
Golden Fleece

Jason sailed in the *Argo*, a special ship, with many other heroes who were called the Argonauts. They had a lot of challenges: they had to fight the harpies and sail between two huge rocks. Jason finally arrived at the home of King Aetes, who gave him some more challenges. Medea, Aetes' daughter, helped Jason to get the fleece. On his way home, he had to escape from the sirens. He got back home, but he never became king.

The Argo

Beasts: (2) _____ (3) _____
(4) _____ (5) _____

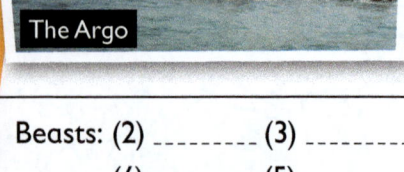

Name of the myth:
(1) _____
_____

Challenges: (7) _____
(8) _____
(9) _____

Hero: (6) _____

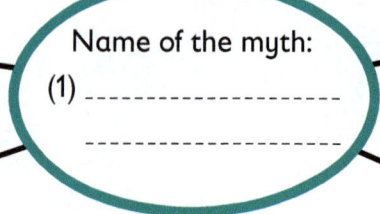

Person who helps: (10) _____

3 Look at the picture and read the story. Complete the sentences about the story. You can use 1, 2, 3, or 4 words.

A long time ago there were two Greek kings. Minos was the king of an island called Crete, and Aegeus was the king of a city called Athens. Minos built an enormous labyrinth on his island. Inside the labyrinth there was a terrible beast that was half man and half bull. It was called the Minotaur.

As part of a prize to Minos, Aegeus had to send some children to Crete every seven years. Minos put the children in the labyrinth, and the Minotaur ate them. Aegeus' son Theseus decided to help the children. He sailed to Crete with the children and killed the Minotaur. Minos' daughter, Ariadne, gave him some string to help him leave the labyrinth.

Before Theseus left Athens, he told his father that if the sail of his ship was white when he came back he was safe, but he forgot to change the color of the sail. When Aegeus saw the black sail, he felt very sad and jumped into the ocean.

1 Minos was the king _____ Crete.
2 The Minotaur lived in King Minos' _____ .
3 Every seven years the Minotaur _____ children from Athens.
4 King Minos had a daughter. Her _____ Ariadne.
5 Theseus didn't remember _____ of the sail.
6 Aegeus jumped into the ocean because _____ .

Project

Invent and write a myth. Make a book.

You need:
- Paper
- 1 sheet of thin cardboard
- Colored markers
- Stapler

How to write the myth and make the book:
1 Think about these questions:
   What special things can your hero do?
   What does your beast look like?
2 Make a diagram like the one on page 16.
3 Fold the thin cardboard in half. Staple the paper inside to make your book.
4 Write your story with a beginning, a middle, and an end.
5 Write the title and draw a picture on the front.

2 Tomorrow's world

🔦 **Show what you know!** What transport words can you remember?

Listening 1 🎵23 Listen and check (✓) the transport words you hear.

2 🎵24 Listen again and correct the sentences.
1 Maria's making a car. (Maria's making a rocket.)
2 Alex thinks we'll travel by bike.
3 The rocket will swim.
4 The rocket will go to the stars.
5 Maria will get some rocket pictures.
6 Their next ezine will be about the transport of the past.

3 Read and order the words.
1 the / hit / will / rocket / The / window.
2 fly? / Maria's / Will / rocket
3 stars. / won't / to / the / rocket / go / Maria's
4 will / hit? / rocket / the / What
5 another / won't / rocket / fly / back yard. / the / They / in
6 transport / be / of / future. / will / the / Rockets / the

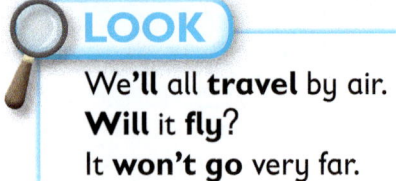

LOOK
We'll all **travel** by air.
Will it **fly**?
It **won't go** very far.

4 **Read and say the words.**

Transport of the future!
It'll be a (1) , not a (2) .
It'll pick up kids for school.
It'll stop for all of us.

Transport of the future!
I'll have a computer on my (3) .
It'll say, "Be careful! (4) on right!"
So I'll ride it where I like!

Transport of the future!
There won't be (5)  or (6) .
How'll we go on vacation?
We'll catch spaceships and spaceplanes.

Transport of the future!
We'll have wings on all our (7) .
Where do you think we'll go?
We'll fly up to the stars.

Transport of the future!
We'll take a (8)  to the Moon.
When'll we leave planet Earth?
We'll leave here very soon!

5 🎵 **Listen and check. Sing the song.**

6 **Read and answer.**

In the future we won't drive on roads and highways. We'll use carplanes, which will fly three meters above the ground. These will carry six people. They won't have a pilot because a computer will fly them. There'll be a small round table and six armchairs with cushions inside, like a small living room. There'll be TV and computer screens to watch our favorite movies or chat on the Internet. There won't be any normal doors. The sides of the carplane will open by moving slowly down under the floor of the car. There won't be any maps, and we'll never get lost because carplanes will always know where to go.

1 What'll we drive in the future?
2 How high will carplanes fly?
3 How many people will a carplane carry?
4 Why won't a carplane have a pilot?
5 Will there be a round table or a square one?
6 What kind of chairs will there be inside?

7 **What do you think? Say "yes" or "no."**

In 2050 ...
1 ... people will eat different food.
2 ... children won't need to go to school.
3 ... everyone will have a computer at home.
4 ... robots will cook and clean for us.
5 ... no one will drive a car.
6 ... people won't use supermarkets.
7 ... people won't have TVs.
8 ... people will wear different clothes.

8 **Work in pairs. Talk about what life will be like in 2050.**

(I think we'll eat different food.)

(Really? What kind of food do you think we'll eat?)

9 **Imagine it's 2050. Write about your bedroom.**

Reading

10 Read and imagine. You have a lot of money. Where will you travel?

http://www.cambridge.org/elt/kidsbox/ezine

Kid's Box Ezine!

home | reports | games | world | email

⭐ Our next ezine is about space travel.

Kid's Box reports — Space Travel

The most famous space agencies in the world are NASA (in the U.S.A.), ESA (Europe), and the Russian and Chinese space programs. They build rockets and teach astronauts how to fly them. Rockets take a long time to build and cost a lot of money. They're too expensive to use as normal transport because they can only fly once. ESA is trying to build the first "spaceplane." This is exciting because it's the way we'll travel in the future. Engineers think their new spaceplane will be cheaper and easier to build and use. People will use them to go to space stations in 2019.

Right now, space tourists can visit the Russian space station Mir, but it's very expensive. In 2001 American businessman Dennis Tito paid $20 million to go for ten days. Some people think there will be different spaceplanes for tourists soon. They will fly higher than 100 km above Earth, the line where space starts. Flights will be two and a half hours, and there will be a pilot and five or six passengers. The passengers will see Earth from above, but they won't go to the Moon. For about five minutes they'll feel like they don't weigh anything, and they will float inside the spaceplane. A ride in these spaceplanes will be cheaper than going to the Mir space station. It'll only cost $200,000!

space | air | Earth | rocket | Moon | astronaut | engineer | businessman | tourist

11 🎵 Listen. Repeat the word. Is it a job? Say "yes" or "no." ▶ 1 Air. (Air – no.)

12 Read again and answer.

1 Which are the most famous space agencies?
2 Name two problems with rockets.
3 Who flies rockets?
4 What is ESA trying to build?
5 When will the spaceplane be ready?
6 Who went into space in 2001?
7 How much did it cost him?
8 How many passengers will travel in a spaceplane?

13 Listen and write the words.

14 Look at the pictures. Complete the sentences. Use words from Activity 13.

1 space

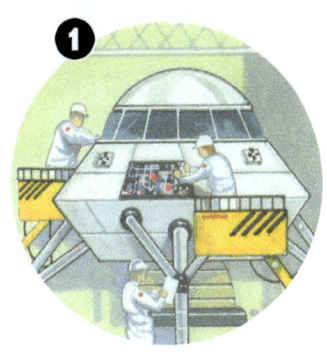   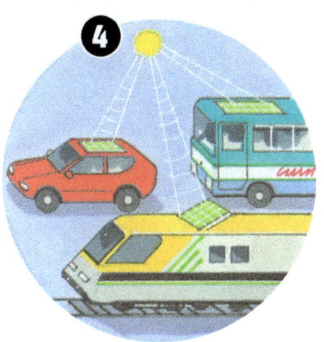

1 _____ will design and make spaceships.
2 _____ will stay in space hotels for their vacations.
3 Robots will work on the _____ , but not on the Sun.
4 _____ and other transport will use solar energy.

15 Listen and answer. What does the man's store sell?

16 Listen again and write.

Booking a space vacation

Name: (1) Robert
Last name: (2) _____
Job: (3) _____
Name of Robert's store: (4) _____
Dream vacation: flying (5) _____
Age next birthday: (6) _____

17 Write questions with "will."

1 When / go / space?
2 What kind of clothes / wear / space?
3 What kind of food / eat / space?
4 What / take / picture of?
5 Who / go with?
6 What / take / with you?

1 When will you go into space?

18 Ask and answer.

(When will you go into space?) (Well, I think I'll go next year.)

19 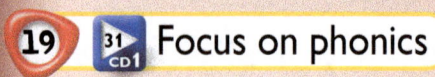 **Focus on phonics**

In the future **we'll** live on Mars,
We'll drive around in flying cars.
I'll have a robot that cooks and plays;
I'm sad I **don't** have that robot today!

20 Listen to these sentences. Say "now" or "the future."

1 We'll use rockets to travel.   The future.

Speaking **21** Imagine your future. Ask and answer about the year 2050.

How old'll you be in 2050?   I'll be 45.

1 How old / be?
2 Where / live?
3 Who / live with?
4 Where / work?

5 What job / do?
6 How / go to work?
7 How / talk to your friends?
8 Where / go for your vacations?

Writing **22** Write about your future.

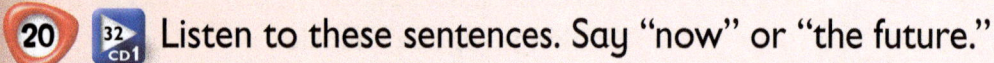
In 2050 I'll be 45 years old. I'll ...

 Joke Corner

Where'll you find a space rocket?

The place where you lost it!

Science | The solar system

FACT: On Jupiter a day lasts only 9 hours and 55 minutes!

1 Read and match the titles with the paragraphs.

| The Sun | Days and years | The planets | Moons |

(1) ----------------------------

We live on a planet, called Earth. There are seven other planets that go around, or orbit, the Sun in our solar system. The Sun is the star at the center of our solar system. It is made of very hot gases, which give us all our natural light and heat. It is about five billion years old and about 145 million km from Earth!

(2) ----------------------------

The eight planets in our solar system are Mercury, Venus, Earth, Mars, Jupiter, Saturn, Uranus, and Neptune. Pluto is a smaller planet, called a dwarf planet. There are two other dwarf planets: Ceres and Eris. You can use a sentence to help you remember the order of the planets from the Sun.

Michael's **V**ery **E**xciting **M**onster, **J**orgut, **S**ometimes **U**nderstands **N**ewspapers.

(3) ----------------------------

Earth has a moon. A moon is like a planet, but it doesn't orbit the Sun. It orbits the planet. Earth's moon isn't the only moon in our solar system. For example, Saturn has 18 moons, and Jupiter has more than 60 moons.

(4) ----------------------------

All of the planets orbit the Sun, but at different speeds. The time it takes a planet to orbit the Sun is a "planetary year." For Earth, that is 365.26 days. Planets orbit the Sun, but at the same time they turn around, or spin. When our part of Earth is facing the Sun, we have daytime, but when Earth turns around, we have night. The time it takes a planet to spin completely is what we call a day. On Earth a day is 24 hours, but on Saturn it is 18.2 hours. The planet with the longest day is Venus. A day on Venus takes 243 Earth days!

2 Find the answers.

1. How many planets are there?
2. Does the Sun orbit Earth?
3. How old is the Sun?
4. How long is a day on Saturn?
5. What's at the center of our solar system?
6. Which planet is closest to the Sun?
7. Are there more moons or planets?
8. Which is longer: a day on Earth or a day on Venus?

3 🎧 Listen and complete the chart.

2,871   57.9   12,104   142,796   ~~149.6~~   1,427

Planet	How far is it from the Sun?	What is its diameter?
Mercury	(a) _____ million km	4,878 km
Venus	108.2 million km	(b) _____ km
Earth	(c) 149.6 million km	12,756 km
Mars	227.9 million km	6,787 km
Jupiter	778.3 million km	(d) _____ km
Saturn	(e) _____ million km	120,660 km
Uranus	(f) _____ million km	51,118 km
Neptune	3,674.5 million km	48,600 km

4 Ask and answer. Check your answers.

How far is Mercury from the Sun?

Fifty-seven point nine million kilometers.

5 Write some quiz questions for a "Class Planet Quiz."

Which is the biggest planet?
Is Venus bigger than Mars?

Project   Make a solar system mobile.

You need:
- Cardboard (thin and thick)
- Scissors
- Colors
- String
- Scotch tape

How to make the solar system mobile:

1 Look at the chart in Activity 3 that tells you how big the planets are.
2 Cut circles of thin cardboard for each planet and the Sun. Color them the same as on page 24.
3 Cut a big circle from the thick cardboard.
4 Make a hole in the middle and knot a piece of string through it.
5 Use string and Scotch tape to hang the Sun and the planets from the big circle, with the Sun in the center.
6 Hang the planets in the correct order with Mercury closest to the Sun. Use the whole circle. Don't put them all in a line because your mobile won't balance!

Review Units 1 and 2

1 Read the text. Choose the right words and write them on the lines.

The Moon is (1) _Earth's_ only natural satellite. That means that the Moon (2) _____ around Earth once every 27 days. It is (3) _____ than Earth, and (4) _____ diameter is 3,474 km.

The first visit to the Moon was (5) _____ July 21, 1969, (6) _____ Neil Armstrong, an American astronaut, (7) _____ the first man to walk on the Moon. The U.S.A. sent rockets with astronauts to the Moon over three years, but they stopped in 1972 because it was very expensive.

Now different space agencies (8) _____ they will send astronauts to the Moon again. The American, the Russian, the Chinese, the Indian, and the European space agencies all have plans for missions to the Moon. NASA (9) _____ to build a camp at one of the lunar poles. They are doing tests in Antarctica to see how well it (10) _____ . It wants astronauts to visit the Moon again, so they can plan to fly to Mars!

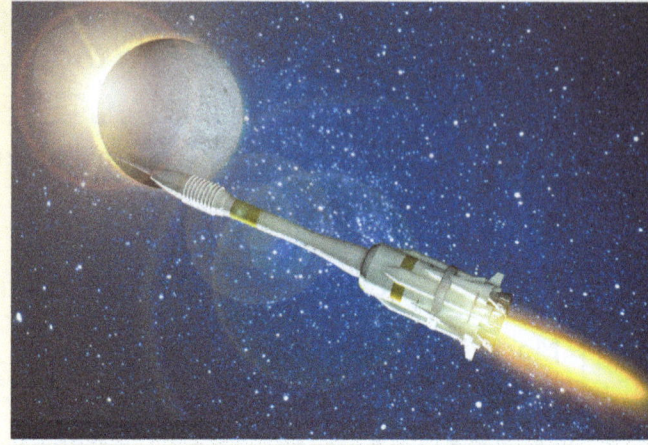

1	Earth	Earth's	Earth is
2	goes	went	go
3	more small	small	smaller
4	it's	its	her
5	in	for	on
6	when	who	where
7	is	was	were
8	say	says	saying
9	can	will	wants
10	works	work	working

2 🎧 37 CD1 Listen and color and write. There is one example.

The planets and

26

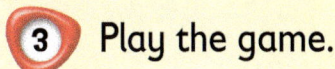

3 Play the game.

Rocket launch

Instructions

- English is the international language of space. USE it or MISS a turn!
- Roll a die and move around the board. First collect a rocket, fuel, and food on Earth.
- When you have all three, continue to the LAUNCH square and fly to the Moon.
- When you reach the LAUNCH square, fly to Mars. How will **you** help the planet?
- Read and follow all the instructions as you move around the board. Race to the END!

3 The great outdoors

🔦 **Show what you know!** What country words can you remember?

Listening 1 🎧 Listen and check (✓) the country words you hear.

2 🎧 Listen again. Say "yes" or "no."

1 Dan broke his arm last week. — No.
2 Alex fell when he was jumping over a rock.
3 Alex was jumping over a rock when he broke his arm.
4 They were walking across a bridge when Alex broke his arm.
5 Alex put his foot in a hole when he was crossing the bridge.
6 Alex was taking his boots off when he broke his arm.

3 Read and choose the right words.

1 Alex and his dad **was** / **were** climbing a hill.
2 Alex **was** / **wasn't** playing when he fell over.
3 They **were walking** / **walks** across a bridge when Alex put his foot in a hole.
4 They **wasn't** / **weren't** having a picnic in the wood.
5 Alex didn't break his arm when he **is** / **was** crossing the bridge.
6 He **was taking** / **took** his boots off when he fell over.

🔍 **LOOK**

I **was jumping** over a rock when I fell.
Were you **playing** when you broke your arm?
No, I **wasn't playing**.

4 Read and complete.

| and I had to jump out   It didn't make a sound   go down a waterfall |
| ~~There was nowhere else to go~~   was racing after me |

I was climbing up the mountain when it started to snow.
I hid in a cave. (1) There was nowhere else to go.
What an adventure!

I was swimming down a river when I thought I saw a tree.
A big crocodile (2) _____.
What an adventure!

I was flying over an island. I was looking all around
When my plane coughed and stopped, (3) _____.
What an adventure!

I was sailing in a river, enjoying it all.
Then I saw a boat in front of me (4) _____.
What an adventure!

I was camping in the jungle. I was sleeping on the ground
When suddenly I felt a snake. (5) _____.
What an adventure! (x3)

5 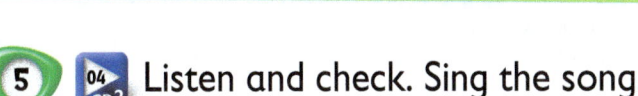 Listen and check. Sing the song.

6 Say what happened next. Discuss.

7 Play the game.

1 Listen to your teacher. Write your answer at the top of a piece of paper.

2 Fold the paper and pass it to the student on your left.

3 You can read the story when you answer the last question.

8 Write the story from the game.

Reading

9 Read and think. Which journey do you think is the most exciting? Why?

http://www.cambridge.org/elt/kidsbox/ezine

Kid's Box Ezine!

home | reports | games | world | email

We always want to find out more about the planet where we live. Explorers travel to new places to learn new things.

Kid's Box reports — Explorers

Marco Polo

Marco Polo was not the first European to travel east to China, but he is the most famous because of his books. A lot of people have read these, including the explorer Christopher Columbus. Marco left Italy in 1271 with his father and uncle, who were making their second journey to China. He went with them and didn't return for 24 years. When they went to China they traveled mostly over land, going through mountains and across the Gobi Desert. When he came west, back to Europe, he traveled more by ocean. He visited India and Sri Lanka before he got back home. He brought back a lot of stories and the idea of paper money, which people later copied.

Ranulph Fiennes

Guinness World Records described Fiennes as "the world's greatest living explorer." He has been on more than 30 expeditions. In 1979, he started an expedition around the world that took three years to finish. He and his team went to both the North and South poles – an adventure of more than 83,000 km. Another difficult expedition was when he walked across Antarctica in 1993 with Dr. Stroud. On this expedition, they didn't carry backpacks on their backs. They pulled sleds that weighed 225 kg because they were carrying all the things that they needed to camp. They had special clothes, tents, sleeping bags, and flashlights to see in the dark.

north | south | east | west | explorer | tent | flashlight | backpack | sleeping bag | camp

10 Listen. Repeat the word and say "Marco," "Ranulph," or "Both." ▶ 1 East.

East. That's "Marco."

11 Read again and correct the sentences.

1 Marco Polo traveled east to Australia.
2 He wrote a newspaper about his journey.
3 Fiennes is the world's greatest soccer player.
4 A backpack is a bag you can sleep in.
5 Fiennes went to India with Dr. Stroud.
6 Their sleds weighed 25 kilos.

12 Read and match. Say the word and the letter.

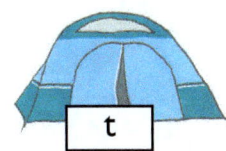 t    u   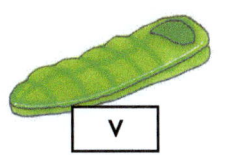 v    w    x

(flashlight – w)

1 It's something you use to see in the dark.
2 It's a big bag that you carry on your back.
3 It's like a small house. You use it when you go camping.
4 It's something that you sleep in.
5 It's someone who travels to a new place to learn about it.

13 Look at the map. Say "yes" or "no."

1 Clidditch is north of Ness Lake.
2 Alchester is south of the Deep Sea.
3 Mainwitch is east of the Deep Sea.
4 Hamptonville is north of Deer Wood.
5 Clidditch is south of Littleton.
6 Oldbridge is east of the mountains.
7 The mountains are south of Mainwitch.
8 Littleton is west of Mainwitch.

14 Play the game.

(It's south of Clidditch and west of Oldbridge.)

(Is it Ness Lake?)

(Yes!)

15 Listen. What camping things do you pick up? Where are you?

16 Write an adventure. Use the map and as many words in the box as you can.

river	grass	bridge	lake
rock	cave	mountain	hill
waterfall	beach	plant	

One day I was walking close to the Black Caves by myself when …

17 **Focus on phonics**

Kate was a cat, and Greg was a goat.
The cat had a hat; the goat had a coat.
Kate could count, but Greg forgot;
The cat was smart, but the goat was not.

Speaking **18** Make questions. Ask and answer.

Were you watching TV at seven o'clock yesterday?

	How many people ... yesterday?	Names
1	were watching TV at *seven* o'clock	Sally, Tim
2	were doing their homework at ... o'clock	
3	were sleeping at ... o'clock	
4	were having lunch at ... o'clock	
5	were walking at ... o'clock	
6	were playing outside at ... o'clock	

Writing **19** Write a report about your class.

I spoke to ten people in my class about their day yesterday. At seven o'clock, two of them were watching TV, but at half past eleven, no one was watching TV!

Joke Corner

Why did the polar bear go to the South Pole?

To see Aunt Arctica!

Art: Landscape painting

FACT: Vincent van Gogh only sold one painting when he was alive.

1 Talk in pairs. What can you see in this painting?

This painting is called *Flatford Mill*, by John Constable, and it is a very famous example of landscape art. Landscape art shows things like mountains, hills, trees, rivers, streams, and woods. The artists usually include the sky in the picture and sometimes the weather, too.

(John Constable *Flatford Mill* "Scene on a Navigable River" 1816–1817 © Tate)

2 Read and complete.

| behind | ~~country~~ | were | beautiful | Artists | outside |

The ancient Chinese, Greeks, and Romans painted the (1) **country** in their pictures, but they put the people in front, and the country was always (2) _____ .

In the 18th century, landscape painting became popular as a kind of art. (3) _____ tried to copy nature exactly in their paintings. Two of the first landscape artists were the English painters John Constable and JMW Turner. They were different from earlier painters because they painted their pictures (4) _____ and not inside a studio. Because of this, their paintings showed a lot of differences in light and color.

From the 1860s a group of French artists called the impressionists continued and added to this style. They started to paint with small spots that gave an "impression" or idea of what they (5) _____ painting. Monet, Pissarro, and Renoir were three famous impressionists who painted (6) _____ landscapes.

The artists who came after the impressionists, called the post-impressionists, included van Gogh and Gauguin. These artists used bright colors. They were different from the impressionists because they used different brush styles to show their feelings. Look at the clouds in the paintings on page 35. Which artist do you think wasn't happy?

3 Read again and answer.

1. When did landscape art become popular?
2. Who were the most important English landscape artists?
3. Where did they paint their pictures?
4. How did the impressionists paint?
5. What kind of colors did van Gogh and Gauguin use?
6. How were they different from the impressionists?

4 Look at these landscape paintings. Which is your favorite?

5 🎧 Listen. Which painting is it?

6 Play the game. Choose a picture. Ask and answer.

Can you see any trees?

Yes, I can.

Project

Draw a landscape picture. Write about it.

You need:
- Colored pencils
- Wax crayons
- Paints

How to draw and write about the landscape picture:

1 Choose words and draw a landscape picture.
2 Make two copies of the same picture.
3 Use different materials to color each picture: Colored pencils, watercolor paints, and wax crayons.
4 Write about your three pictures. Use the text opposite and answer these questions:
- Which material is the easiest to use? Why?
- Which picture is the brightest?
- Which do you like the best? Why?

There's a $\frac{\text{small wood}}{\text{big forest}}$ in the middle of my landscape picture. On the $\frac{\text{left}}{\text{right}}$ of this, there's a $\frac{\text{lake}}{\text{river}}$. On the other side there's a field with $\frac{\text{sheep}}{\text{cows}}$ eating grass in it. In the background we can see $\frac{\text{hills}}{\text{mountains}}$.

In front of the trees, in the middle, you can see a $\frac{\text{man}}{\text{woman}}$ who is $\frac{\text{carrying a backpack}}{\text{holding a map}}$. There are a lot of $\frac{\text{flowers}}{\text{leaves}}$ on the ground. It's $\frac{\text{hot and sunny}}{\text{cold and cloudy}}$.

35

4 Food, glorious food!

Show what you know! What food words can you remember?

Listening 1 Listen and check (✓) the food words you hear.

2 Listen again. Who said it?

1 We'll make Tarte Tatin next Wednesday afternoon. — The teacher.
2 I think we have too many apples.
3 We have three kilos of sugar, too. We have too much!
4 Do we have enough flour?
5 So we don't have enough eggs either.
6 We have too much sugar and too many apples.

3 Read and order the words.

1 apples. / a / bag / Maria has / of / big
2 many / They have / apples. / too
3 a / They have / flour. / little
4 don't have / flour. / We / enough
5 one / only / They have / egg.
6 flour or / enough / don't have / They / eggs.

LOOK

You'll need **enough** apples to cover the base.
We don't have **enough** eggs.   Do we have **enough** flour?
We have **too many** apples.   We have **too much** sugar.

4 🎧 **Listen and check (✓) the box.**

1 What does Michael want in his coffee?

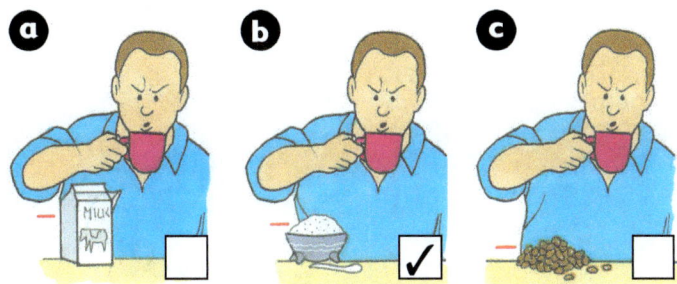

2 What did Paul put on the table?

3 What does Robert want on his pasta?

4 What did Mary put on the table?

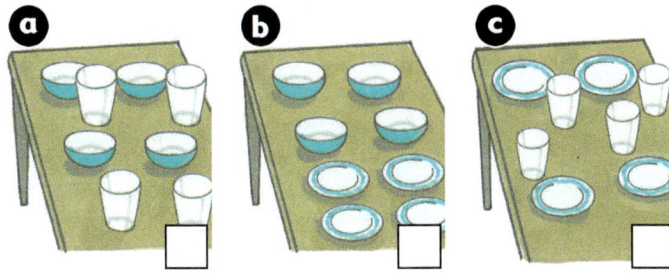

5 How many pizzas did Emma cook?

5 **Look. Correct the sentences.**

1 There are too many knives.
2 There aren't enough spoons.
3 There are too many pizzas.
4 There isn't enough milk.
5 There are too many peas.
6 There isn't enough strawberry ice cream.

6 **Ask your friend ten questions. Use these words. Write your friend's answers.**

candy	chocolate	pizza
vegetables	salads	fruit
cheese	strawberries	soup
pasta	fish	eggs	meat

How often do you eat candy? — Twice a day.

How often do you eat fish? — Three times a week.

7 **Talk with your friend.**

I think I eat too much candy. What do you think?

I think you eat too much candy, too … and I …

8 **Tell the rest of the class.**

We think we don't eat enough fruit because we only have fruit once a day …

Reading **9** Read and think. Which of these don't have sugar?

http://www.cambridge.org/elt/kidsbox/ezine

Kid's Box Ezine!

home | reports | games | world | email

People from different countries eat different kinds of food. Some dishes are famous all over the world.

Kid's Box reports Food

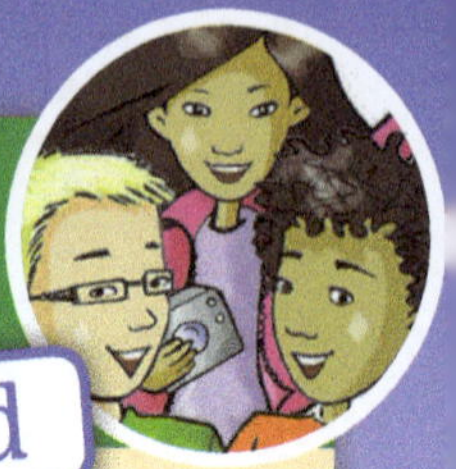

a

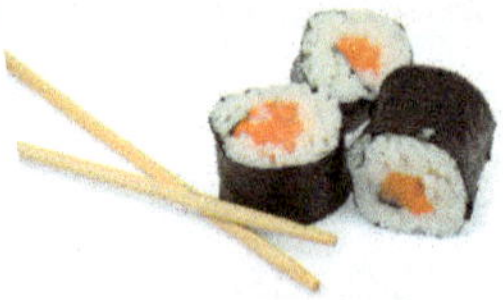

Sushi is a cold Japanese dish. You can make sushi with rice and fish that isn't cooked. You eat sushi with chopsticks.

b

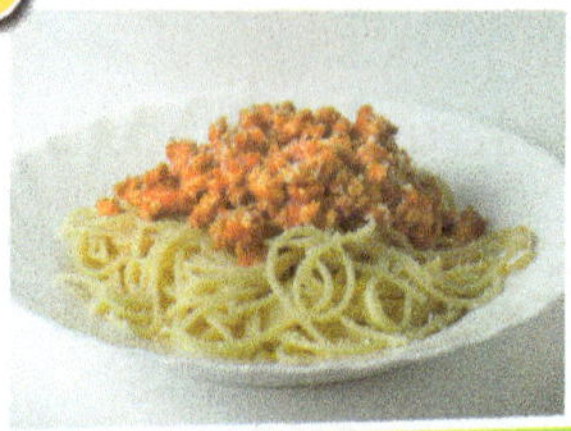

In Italy they eat a lot of pizzas and pasta dishes. There are a lot of different kinds of pasta and sauces. Two of the most famous are spaghetti and macaroni.

c

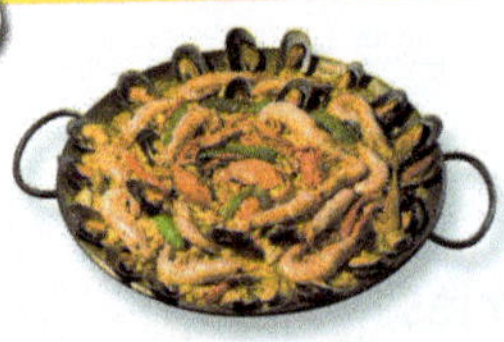

Paella is Spanish. It's a rice dish and also the name of the pan you use. People make it with chicken or seafood. It's delicious!

d

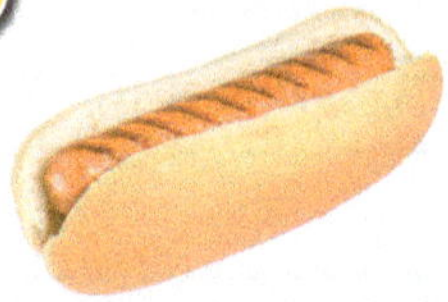

What's your favorite snack between meals? The hot dog – a sausage in a long bread roll – is famous all over the world.

e

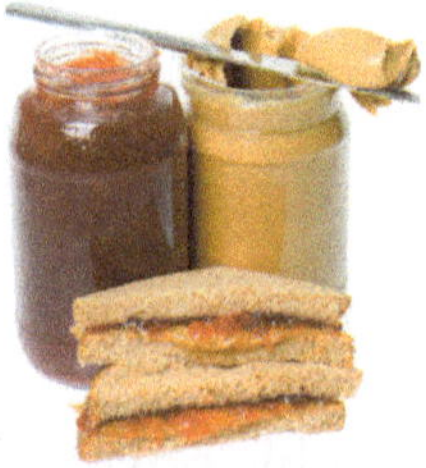

Peanut butter and jelly sandwiches are popular in the U.S.A. Butter is made from milk and peanut butter is made from peanuts, of course. We cook fruit and sugar at a high temperature to make jelly.

f

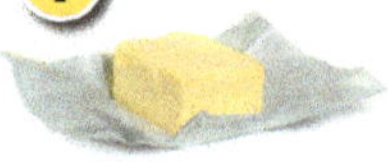

g

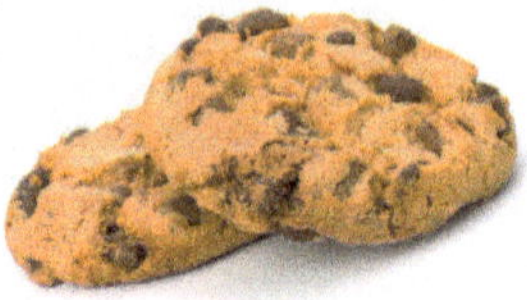

Do you eat cookies as a snack? In the U.K. cookies are called biscuits. Cookies can have chocolate, dry fruit, or jelly in them. They have sugar, too.

h

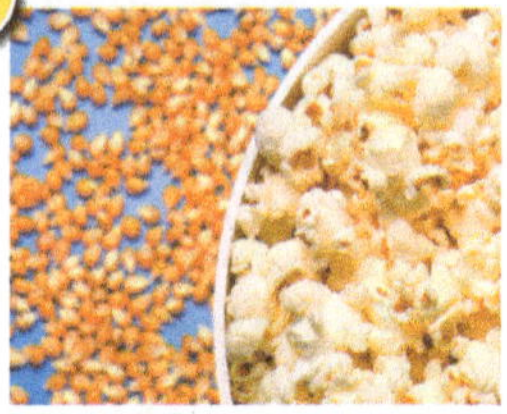

Popcorn is a healthier snack. The corn seeds make a loud noise in the pan. People ate popcorn more than 2,000 years ago. Today people often eat it at the movies with salt, or with sugar and butter.

butter | cookie | chopsticks | jelly | snack | pan | sauce | popcorn

10 17 CD2 Listen. Repeat the word and say the letter.

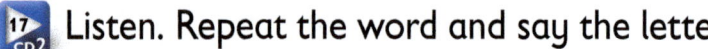

1 Sauce. — Sauce. That's "b."

11 Read again and say "yes" or "no."

1 Sushi is a Japanese dish.
2 Sushi is made from eggs and bread.
3 Paella is the name of a dish and a pan.
4 Peanut butter and jelly sandwiches are popular in North America.
5 A snack is a heavy meal at lunchtime.
6 Butter is made from milk.
7 Jelly is made from fruit and peanuts.
8 *Biscuit* is another word for "cookie."

12 Listen and write the words.

13 Read and order the pictures.

"I feel hungry.
What can I eat?"
  "Cheese and salad.
  Fish and meat.
  Not too many cookies,
  You know it's not good.
  Eat fruit and vegetables –
  You know you should.

  You can eat with chopsticks,
  A knife, fork, or spoon."
"I eat snacks with my fingers.
Oh! Let's eat soon!"
  "There's a pan of pasta
  Or a bowl of rice."
"Or a big Italian pizza.
Mmm! That's nice!
Is there any peanut butter?
Is that strawberry jelly?
Are you going to make a sandwich?"
  "Yes, I am."
"Oooh! Thanks, Dad!"

14 Listen and sing the song.

15 Write four sentences. Use the words in the boxes. Play *Food bingo*.

| There's too much | There are too many |
| There isn't enough | There aren't enough |

jelly	butter	salt	pepper	pasta
rice	cookies	hot dogs	chopsticks
snacks	burgers	sandwiches	olives

1 pan

16 Read and write the right words.

Last Saturday Katy decided to make Spaghetti Bolognese, her favorite (1) **Italian** pasta (2) _____.

First she put some cold water and some (3) _____ into a big pan to boil.

When the water was (4) _____, she put the spaghetti into it to cook.

While this was cooking, she made the (5) _____ for it. She (6) _____ some onions with meat and (7) _____. She added some (8) _____, but she put in (9) _____!

When it was ready, she put the spaghetti onto a big plate and put the sauce on top. When she put her (10) _____ into her mouth to taste it, it was horrible.

1	French	Spanish	~~Italian~~
2	plate	dish	bowl
3	tea	jelly	salt
4	hot	corn	cold
5	snack	sandwich	sauce
6	cooks	cooked	cooking
7	bananas	tomatoes	ice cream
8	sugar	salt	jelly
9	too many	enough	too much
10	flash drive	fork	cup

17 Invent a story about food. Give words for your friend to choose.

18 Focus on phonics

Night rhymes with **right** and **light**,
Laugh with **half** and **cough** with **off**.
But **enough** rhymes with **puff**,
And **through** with **who** and **you**!

Speaking **19** Imagine you're at an international party. Ask and answer.

Would you like some sushi, Richard?   Yes, please.
Would you like a hot dog, Lucy?   No, thank you.

Names	sushi	hot dog	paella	cookie	spaghetti	popcorn	olive
Me	✗	✓	✓	✓	✗	✗	✓
Richard	✓						
Lucy		✗					
Emma							

Writing **20** Copy the chart and write about your answers.

In my group, three of us wanted sushi and four of us wanted some cookies. No one wanted any popcorn ...

Joke Corner

What do cats like to eat?

Mice cream!

Science: Micro-organisms

FACT: The holes in Swiss cheese are because of the gas made by bacteria.

1 Read and match the words with pictures a–d.

Micro-organisms – smaller than a hair
Micro-organisms are very small living things, so we must use a **microscope** to see them. Two important kinds of micro-organisms are bacteria and fungus. Some micro-organisms are bad for our health, but others are good for us.

Micro-organisms that are bad for us
Some food (especially meat) can have bacteria. Bacteria can't live in food that we cook thoroughly, but if you eat food that isn't cooked thoroughly, the bacteria can make you very sick. **Bacteria** grow best at warm temperatures. That's why we keep a lot of food in the fridge.

Mold is a micro-organism that grows on food. It can make you sick if you eat it.

We all have bacteria in our mouths. This is why we brush our teeth after every meal.

Health tips about micro-organisms that we don't want
You can stop passing unhealthy micro-organisms from one place to another if you do these things.

1 Wash your hands with soap before you eat, after you touch food, and after you go to the bathroom.
2 Cover your mouth when you cough.
3 If you are sick, don't go where there are a lot of people.
4 Don't eat food that is not fresh or not cooked thoroughly.
5 Keep uncooked meat away from other food in the fridge.

Micro-organisms that are good for us
Some micro-organisms are important for our body and for making some foods. For example, we use a micro-organism called yeast when we make bread. **Yeast** makes the bread mixture grow when we cook it. We also use a different micro-organism, or bacteria, to make yogurt.

2 Choose the best title for the text.

Be careful with yeast ☐   Micro-organisms help us and hurt us ☐   Cheese is good for you ☐

3 Read again and choose the right answer.

1 Micro-organisms are …
 A all good.   B all bad.
 C sometimes good and sometimes bad.
2 To stop bacteria passing from one person to another when we cough we must …
 A cover our mouth.   B have clean shoes.
 C not watch TV.
3 These micro-organisms are bad for us.
 A Yeast   B Mold on fruit
 C Bacteria in yogurt
4 We use yeast …
 A to make yogurt.   B to make bread.
 C to make ice cream.
5 This is not a micro-organism.
 A Bacteria   B Yeast   C Bread

4 Read and complete.

different   smell   kind
~~goats~~   bacteria   milk
quickly   makes   prefer
began   hard   years

5 Read again and answer.
1 Where do we get milk from?
2 Where do we keep milk cold?
3 When do lumps form in milk?
4 What different things can we make from milk?
5 What changes milk into yogurt?
6 What bacteria do people usually use to make hard cheese?

Milk, yogurt, and cheese

We get milk from cows, sheep, and (1) goats____. If you leave a glass of (2) _____ out of your fridge on a hot day, it changes (3) _____. Small solid lumps start to form on the top of it. This is because (4) _____ in the air go into the milk and change it into yogurt. Some kinds of bacteria can be bad for you or make the milk (5) _____ bad, but if your milk has the right (6) _____ of bacteria, it (7) _____ yogurt. Yogurt tastes good, and it is healthy, but you need to keep it in the fridge.
People tried using (8) _____ kinds of bacteria with milk, and then they (9) _____ to make cheese. They usually use bacteria called rennet to make hard cheese. People keep some of these cheeses for three or four (10) _____ or more because they like the taste of old cheese. What kind of cheese do you like, (11) _____ cheese or soft cheese? Do you (12) _____ cheese made from sheep's, goat's, or cow's milk? What's the difference in taste?

Project  Make some soft cheese.

You need:
- 2 liters of yogurt
- 1 small spoon of salt
- Clean thin cloth
- 2 bowls
- Fork or whisk

How to make the soft cheese:
There are a lot of different kinds of cheese, all of which are made from milk with bacteria. It's easier to make cheese from yogurt because it has live bacteria in it. If you can't do this at school, maybe you can do it at home.

1 Put the yogurt in a bowl and mix it up so it is smooth.
2 Add a small spoon of salt and mix it again.
3 Put it into the cloth. Lift the four corners and tie a knot in the cloth. Put it over the second bowl so the liquid can fall through the cloth. The "cheese" then stays inside the cloth.
4 After about 24 hours, you can open up the cloth. Form the cheese into a ball and keep it in the fridge. You must eat it in two days.

Review Units 3 and 4

1 25 CD2 Listen and draw lines. There is one example.

Helen   Katy   Harry   Richard   Michael   Sarah   William

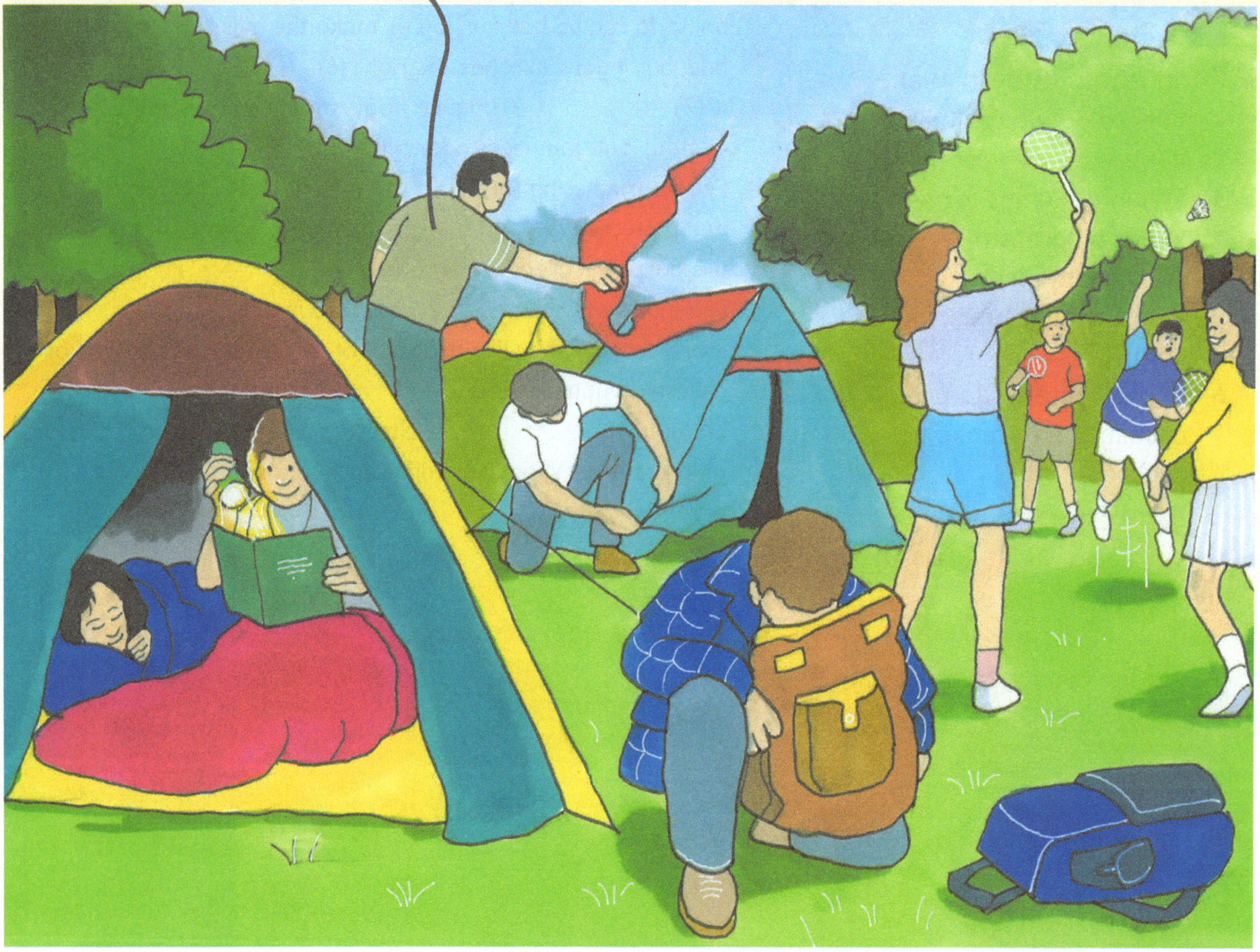

2 Ask and answer.

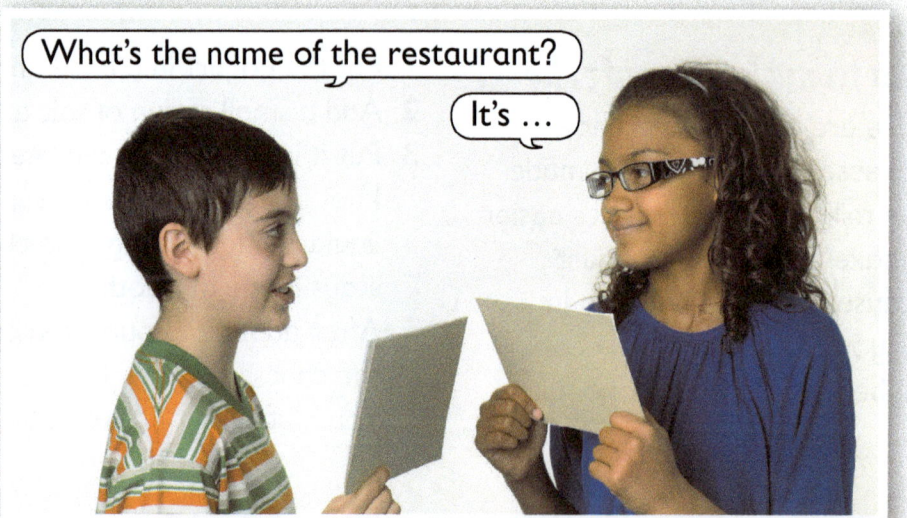

What's the name of the restaurant?
It's …

3 Play the game.

Snakes and ladders

Instructions
- Roll a die and move around the board.
- When you land on a square with words, make a sentence.
- If you are right, go UP the ladder. DON'T go down the snake.
  If you are wrong, DON'T go up the ladder. Go DOWN the snake.

5 Under the ocean

Show what you know! What ocean words can you remember?

Listening 1 Listen and check (✓) the ocean words you hear.

2 Listen again and answer the questions.

1 Have they talked about the next ezine for three weeks or three days? **For three days.**
2 What have the people found on the beach?
3 Have the rescue people been there since ten o'clock or since seven o'clock?
4 What do they think the dolphin has lost?
5 Who hasn't seen a dolphin before?
6 Has the dolphin eaten anything?
7 What have they done to help the dolphin?
8 Has the dolphin been on the sand for 30 minutes or three hours?

3 Read and match.

1 I've never seen
2 The rescue people have been
3 The dolphin has been on the
4 The kids have been at the beach
5 They still haven't
6 We've worked on the

a there for two hours.
b project for three days.
c since half past ten.
d a dolphin before.
e sand since nine o'clock.
f thought of a project.

LOOK
We **still** haven't chosen a project. The rescue people have been here **since** ten o'clock. It's been here **for** about three hours.

4 Read and look at the pictures. Check (✓) the things that he has done.

I've been at the beach since half past three.
I've picked up stones and shells from the sea.
I've walked in the water, and I've touched it with my hand.
I've found tide pools, and I've played with the sand.
I still haven't seen a dolphin or a whale.
I still haven't ridden in a boat with a sail.
I still haven't caught a fish to eat
Or met a mermaid without any feet.
But I've sat on my towel, felt the sun on my face,
And I've thought that this is my favorite place.
I've watched the birds as they've flown in the air.
I've eaten a sandwich, an apple, and a pear.
I've swum with my friends, made castles with my dad.
It's one of the best days that I've ever had!
We've been here for hours, now it's time to go.
I love the beach, that's all I need to know. (x3)

5 Listen and sing the song.

6 Ask and answer.
- Has he played with the sand? — Yes, he has.
- Has he sailed in a boat? — No, he hasn't.

7 Look at Michael's lifeline. Make ten sentences about his life: five with "since" and five with "for."

2006	2009	2012	2014	2015
Michael was born in Los Angeles, California.	Michael's sister, Emma, was born.	Michael started at Beach Street School.	Michael learned to play tennis.	Michael started to study French.

1 Michael / have / sister
   Michael has had a sister since 2009.
2 Michael / live / in Los Angeles
3 Michael / go / Beach Street School
4 Michael / play tennis
5 Michael / study French

8 Draw and write your lifeline. Talk about it with a friend.
- I've lived here since 2014.
- Where did you live before?

Reading 9 Read and think. Which is the smallest animal in the pictures?

Kid's Box Ezine!

home | reports | games | world | email

Kid's Box reports — Sea animals

We still haven't explored our seas and oceans completely, but here are some interesting sea animals.

a Seals live in the ocean and on land, like turtles, but they don't lay eggs! They are mammals, so they have babies and feed them milk.

b This giant Japanese spider crab has lived in the ocean since the time of the dinosaurs. It's 4 m across. It has two claws and eight thin legs with white spots.

c Like crabs, lobsters have a hard shell and two big claws, but their bodies aren't round.

d Coral reefs look like forests, but corals aren't plants. Each reef is millions of very small animals. The reefs are important because a lot of other sea animals live there.

e Jellyfish aren't fish. They have been in our seas and oceans for 650 million years. They don't have a brain or bones, and they can be from 2.5 cm to 61 m long. They eat small fish and tiny animals called zooplankton.

f This blue-ringed octopus lives in coral reefs close to Australia. It's very small (6 cm), but it's very dangerous.

g Like an octopus, a squid has eight "legs." This is a giant squid. They can be 14 m long, and they have the biggest eyes in the world.

crab | lobster | seal | coral | jellyfish | octopus | squid

10 Listen. Repeat the word and say the letter. ▶ 1 Lobster. — Lobster. That's "c."

11 Read again and answer.
1 Which of these sea animals is a mammal?
2 Which small animal is very dangerous?
3 Why are coral reefs important?
4 How is a crab different from a lobster?
5 Which animal has the biggest eyes?
6 Which animal can be 61 meters long?

48

12 Correct the sentences.

1 People have eaten lobsters since 2,000 years.
2 Jellyfish lived on Earth for millions of years.
3 People have finded giant squid in all the world's oceans.
4 There have been coral reefs in our oceans since millions of years.
5 Scientists have found 6,000 different kinds of crab, but they still hasn't found them all.
6 Seals have swimmed in our oceans for 22 million years.

13 Listen and write a letter in each box.

What is each person's favorite thing at the aquarium?

14 Read the text and write the missing words. Write one word on each line.

We find coral reefs in warm (1) **water** _____ , usually close to land. They are home to a lot of different sea (2) _____ , like lobsters, turtles, octopuses, and jellyfish. A lot of beautiful (3) _____ live here, too, like the clownfish and the parrotfish. The biggest coral reef (4) _____ the world is the Great Barrier Reef. It is in the ocean close to Australia. Coral reefs (5) _____ in danger because of dirty water and the things some people do. We need (6) _____ take care of our coral reefs.

15 Play the game.

Sam's seen a small squid.

16 **Focus on phonics**

Can you say the words with me?
Bottle, **win**dow, and **mon**key.
Now hear the stress at the end,
To**day**, gi**raffe**, be**low**, a**gain**!

Count the syllables, these have three,
Elephant, **jel**lyfish, **fam**ily.
Stressed at the end, can you hear?
Kanga**roo**, maga**zine**, engi**neer**.

Speaking **17** Ask and answer.

Questionnaire

1 Have you ever heard dolphins on TV?
2 … seen a crab in a restaurant?
3 … eaten lobster?
4 … taken a picture of a dolphin?
5 … had a fish for a pet?
6 … swum in the ocean?
7 … caught an octopus?
8 … listened to a whale's song on CD?

Writing **18** Write eight more questions for your friend to answer. Use the questionnaire to help you.

Joke Corner

What kind of shells will you always find in the ocean?

Wet ones!

Science | Food chains

FACT: Oceans cover almost three quarters of Earth. The different oceans join together to make the biggest habitat on Earth.

1 Read and answer.
1. What is the first thing in every food chain?
2. What is the "top predator" in the text? Think of another one.
3. Which is the predator: krill or whale? Which is the prey?
4. Talk about other problems in food chains. What can we do about them?

We eat fish, but what do fish eat? They eat very, very small plants and animals in the water. Then other fish and animals, including us, eat them. This means that fish are part of a food chain. We can talk about food chains in rivers and oceans or about food chains on land.

Food chains always start with a green plant. In the ocean these very small plants are called phytoplankton (plant plankton). All plants are called **producers** because they make (or "produce") their food. Phytoplankton, like other plants, take energy from the Sun and make it into food. They are at the start of a food chain. Then there are very small animals called zooplankton (animal plankton) that eat the phytoplankton. In a spoonful of ocean water there can be a million phytoplankton and zooplankton. Animals and fish are called **consumers** because they eat (or "consume") other plants and animals.

Look at this simple Antarctic food chain.

phytoplankton

krill

baleen whale

In this chain, the **producer** is the phytoplankton, and the **consumers** are the krill and baleen whale. We also see here an example of prey and predator. A **predator** is an animal that eats another animal. The animal that the predator eats is called the **prey**.

Food chains end with top predators – animals that have no natural enemies. Sharks are examples of top predators.

Food chains are very important because they help us understand how nature lives together. If you take away part of the chain, you change everything in that chain. For example, if you make the water dirty in the oceans, plankton will die. If there is no plankton, the small fish don't have any food to eat. If the small fish don't have any food, the big fish can't eat the small fish, and so the problem goes up the chain.

2 Find these words.
1. very small plants in the ocean =
2. the part of the food chain that makes food =
3. the part of the food chain that eats food =
4. a fish or animal that eats another fish or animal =

Food webs
When all the food chains in a habitat are joined together, they form a food web. This can look very complicated, but it is only a lot of food chains joined together.

3 🎧 36 CD2 Listen and complete the ocean food web.

4 How many food chains can you make from this web? In pairs, draw diagrams like the Antarctic food chain on page 52.

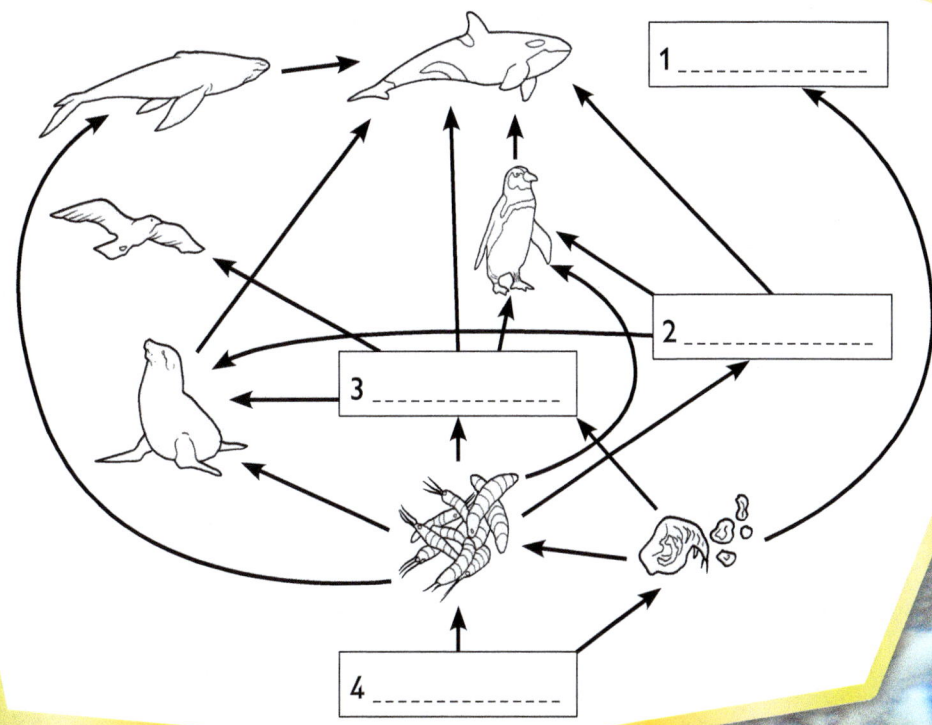

Project

Make a food web poster: Who eats what?

You need:
- Books or the Internet to find information
- Poster paper

How to make the food web poster:
1 Choose a habitat to study (ocean, coral reef, river, land, forest, field, jungle).
2 Think about the animals that live in that habitat and find out about others.
3 Think about what each one eats and find out about others.
4 Write a fact sheet for each animal and draw a picture.
5 Put them on your poster.
6 Join them with arrows, like this:

6 Free time

Show what you know! What free time words can you remember?

Listening 1 🔊 Listen and check (✓) the free time words you hear.

2 🔊 Listen again and correct the sentences.

1 Everything's dry outside.
   (Everything's wet outside.)
2 There's nothing to do on the playground.
3 They have everything they need to play field hockey.
4 Someone else wants to kick the ball.
5 They have to go somewhere else to dance.
6 Now they have something to sing about.

3 Read and choose the right words.

1 **Everything** / **Nothing** is wet outside.
2 There's **nothing** / **anything** to do in the classroom.
3 There's **everywhere** / **nowhere** to play.
4 They don't have **everywhere** / **anywhere** to play Ping-Pong.
5 They have **everything** / **nothing** they need to play.
6 Does **anyone** / **no one** else want to play?
7 Find **nowhere** / **somewhere** else to play.
8 Go outside, **everyone** / **no one**!

LOOK

some	any	no	every
someone	**any**one	**no** one	**every**one
something	**any**thing	**no**thing	**every**thing
somewhere	**any**where	**no**where	**every**where

4 Read and complete.

> anything   everyone   no one
> anyone   anywhere   Someone
> something   ~~somewhere~~   everything
> Everyone

from: alex360@kidsbox.mail

Dear Robert,

Last Saturday we decided to go (1) **somewhere** different. (2) _____ who works with Dad told him about an exciting new exhibit at the Train Museum. (3) _____ knows that trains are old, but we wanted to know which was the first train. There wasn't (4) _____ to ask, but we read some interesting posters.

Richard Trevithick made the first train in 1803, but (5) _____ used the train until 1829 when Robert Stephenson built the Rocket. It was the first real train, and (6) _____ copied the design when they made trains later. We saw a copy of the Rocket in the museum. Here's a picture. Have you ever seen it?

I think we saw (7) _____ in the museum, but we were tired and there wasn't (8) _____ to sit down, so we went to the restaurant. We had (9) _____ to drink before the museum closed at half past five. It was a great day out. What about you? Did you do (10) _____ interesting last weekend?

All the best,
Alex

5 Listen and write.

Kind of show: (1) **quiz show** _____

The two children's names:
(2) _____ and (3) _____

The place: somewhere in the (4) _____

The place: (5) _____

How many questions does the boy ask?
(6) _____

6 Play the game. Say it in ten.

- It's a sport.
- Yes, it is.
- No, it isn't.
- It's something you play with a ball.
- It's something you play in a sports center.

7 Ask and answer.

- Do you like playing Ping-Pong?

Find someone who …	Name
1 likes playing Ping-Pong	Eva
2 goes swimming more than twice a week	
3 has a hobby different from yours	
4 can ski	
5 likes skating	
6 goes somewhere different from you in his/her free time	

Reading

8 Read and think. How many of these can be indoor hobbies?

http://www.cambridge.org/elt/kidsbox/ezine

Kid's Box Ezine! home | reports | games | world | email

Kid's Box reports — Hobbies

This month we've talked with different people about their hobbies.

Harry enjoys fashion design. He makes amazing T-shirts, and a lot of his friends ask him to make T-shirts for them. He sews and paints the T-shirts.

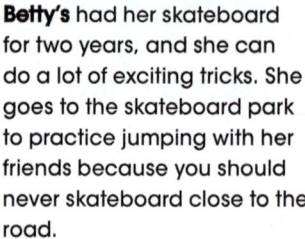

Betty's had her skateboard for two years, and she can do a lot of exciting tricks. She goes to the skateboard park to practice jumping with her friends because you should never skateboard close to the road.

Emma's ridden a bike since she was five. She rides her mountain bike everywhere, but she enjoys it best when she and her dad go to a special bike trail. They can ride up and down hills and through woods.

Sarah loves doing jigsaw puzzles and playing board games. She plays chess in the school club, and she's practicing for a national competition. People have played chess for more than a thousand years.

Robert loves music, but he doesn't play an instrument. He uses his mouth to copy the sounds and rhythms of drums. This is called beatbox.

Richard's very active and strong, and he does free running. He runs, jumps, and climbs walls in downtown areas. Free runners learn to jump and land safely in different ways, but it's still dangerous.

skateboard | fashion design | free running | mountain bike | beatbox | board games | chess | jigsaw puzzles

9 Listen. Repeat the word and say the name.

> 1 Mountain bike.
> Mountain bike. That's Emma.

10 Read again and find these things.

1 somewhere you can go to ride
2 something you can wear
3 somewhere with a lot of trees
4 something you sit on to ride
5 something you stand on to ride
6 something that people have played for centuries

11 Read and complete.

| something | chess | learn | cut | watch | beatbox | ~~hobbies~~ |
| sing | park | somewhere | ski | design | climb | bike | everyone |

Free time, free time. Lots of (1) **hobbies** to do.
There's something for (2) _____. There's (3) _____ for you.

You can do anything in your free time.
You can learn to skate, you can learn to (4) _____.
You can skateboard in a (5) _____ or (6) _____ in the snow.
You can (7) _____ some clothes: draw, (8) _____, and sew.

You can learn to play (9) _____ if that's what you like.
You can learn to sail or ride a mountain (10) _____.
You can learn about music: play it or (11) _____,
Pop, rap, or (12) _____. Enjoy everything.

You can (13) _____ movies or act in a play.
You can walk in the hills and (14) _____ to find your way.
You'll have (15) _____ to go and something to do,
You'll make new friends who like the same things as you.

Chorus

12 Listen and check. Sing the song.

13 Invent another verse. Use these words or your own ideas.

| dance | play soccer / baseball | sled | planes | cars | golf | field hockey |
| tennis | swim | camp | make | take pictures | cook | mix | weigh |

14 Read the definitions. What hobby is it?

1 This is something you can do in your free time. You do it with a board, which is usually made of wood, and you can do it in a special park.
2 This is a sport you can play anywhere and with anyone, but people usually play it in towns or cities. You have to be active and healthy to do this.
3 You can play this anywhere, but you need a board and pieces. People usually sit down when they play this.

15 Write more definitions for your friend to guess.

It's something …
Everyone can …

16 🔊 **Focus on phonics**

I went to L**o**ndon with my c**ou**sin, G**u**s.
It was a lot of f**u**n – j**u**st the two of **u**s.
We had a really y**u**mmy l**u**nch,
Then caught a d**ou**ble-decker b**u**s!

Speaking **17** In groups, ask and answer.

Questionnaire

1 Do you prefer to spend your free time inside or outside?
2 Can you play chess?
3 Do you like music?
4 What board games do you like?
5 Do you have a bike?
6 Have you ever been on a skateboard?
7 What sports do you play?
8 Have you ever hurt your knees or elbows playing sports?
9 What else do you do in your free time? Name three things.

Writing **18** Write about your hobbies and someone with different hobbies.

In my free time, I like to be outside ...
My friend William has different hobbies. In his free time, he ...

 Joke Corner

Why can't you have everything?

Because you have nowhere to put it!

Music | Popular music

FACT: The first CD ever made was by the Swedish pop group ABBA in 1982.

1 Read about music. Now listen. Which piece do you prefer?

2 Match the words with pictures a–e. Read and check.

> rock   rap   jazz
> opera   beatbox

There are a lot of different kinds of music. To talk about them, we can look at the different instruments they use, but we also need to understand some of the different parts of a piece of music.

The **melody** is the tune, or the line of notes that you sing in a song. It is usually the easiest part to remember.

The **tempo** is the speed of the music. If you play music more quickly or more slowly, it changes how the music sounds.

The **harmony** is behind the melody. It changes how the music feels.

Popular music – then and now

The name *pop* music comes from "**popular** music," but do you know what was popular more than 200 years ago? Or 80 years ago? Here are some of the different styles of music.

Opera is a kind of classical music. It's 400 years old but was very popular 200 years ago. An opera is a musical play with an orchestra. The singers wear costumes and tell a story, so there are a lot of different melodies and tempos.

Jazz music combines music from North America and Africa, and many styles have developed since people started playing jazz 100 years ago. One of the most important things in jazz is improvisation. This means that musicians invent the music while they're playing it.

When we say "pop music" now, we think of short songs with a strong rhythm and a melody that is easy to remember. **Rock** music is a kind of pop music that was first very popular in the 1960s and 1970s. The singer sings the melody, and electric and bass guitars play the harmonies. The drums and bass guitars are important for the rhythm.

Rap started more than 20 years ago. Rappers sing or say their rhymes to an electronic rhythm. The melody isn't complicated, and there isn't much harmony.

Beatbox is a new kind of singing. Beatboxers use their mouths and bodies to copy drums and other musical sounds. It's like rap, but there are more sounds than words. Have you tried it?

3 Listen and say "yes" or "no."

4 Listen. Number the kinds of music 1–6.

beatbox ☐   rap ☐   pop ☐   opera [1]   rock ☐   jazz ☐

5 Read and complete.

| CDs | concerts | English | guitar | ~~singer~~ | Spanish | world | problems |

Bruce Springsteen is an important rock (1) **singer** and songwriter from the U.S.A. He sings and plays the (2) _____ and the piano. His songs are often about everyday (3) _____ that people have. He has recorded and performed a lot of his songs with the E Street Band, and together they are famous for their long, exciting (4) _____ . Two of his best albums are *Born in the U.S.A.* and *Born to Run*. He has sold more than 65 million albums in the U.S.A. and has won 18 Grammy Awards for his songs.

Shakira is a pop singer and songwriter from Colombia in South America. She normally sings in (5) _____ or English, but she can also speak two other languages. She has sold more records and (6) _____ than any other Colombian ever and has sold 50 million albums all over the (7) _____ . *Laundry Service* was her first CD in (8) _____ , and it was number three in both the U.S. and British charts.

6 Listen to the beatbox rhythms. Clap and tap.

Project
Make a musical bottle.

You need:
- An empty plastic drink bottle (you don't need the top)
- Scissors
- Scotch tape
- A bowl
- Water

How to make the musical bottle:
1 Cut the bottom off your plastic bottle with scissors. Ask your teacher to help if it is difficult.
2 Cover the edge (where you have cut) with Scotch tape.
3 Put water into the bowl.
4 Put your bottle into the water. You can hit it softly with a pencil or you can try to blow across it.
5 Move the bottle in and out of the water to change the musical note. Whose bottle makes the highest note? Whose bottle makes the lowest note?

Review Units 5 and 6

1. Read the letter and write the missing words. Write one word on each line.

Dear Peter,

1 How are you? In your last letter you asked me about my <u>hobbies</u>, so I'm going to tell you about two of them: chess and my mountain bike.

2 I've played chess _____ four years now. I play with my friends
3 at a club in school. We meet twice a week, _____
4 Tuesdays and Thursdays. I really _____ it because you
5 have _____ think a lot and because there's a lot of action.

6 My other hobby is _____ my mountain bike up to the bike trails close to our house with my brother. I've included a picture of me on my bike.

Tell me about some of your hobbies.

Best wishes,

Robert

2. Look at the pictures. Tell the story.

3 Play the game.

Can you make a question?

Instructions
- Roll a die and move around the board.
- You must win three verbs in a line: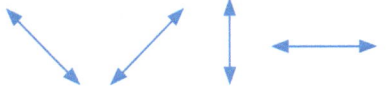

- To win a verb, make a correct sentence using the verb in the present perfect tense.
  - I've visited Grandma twice this week.
- When you get a verb, cover it with a piece of paper and write your sentence down.
- You can land on a square that someone else has won, but you can't win it, too!

40 dance	39 sail	38 snow	37	36 comb
31 ski	32 dream	33 plant	34 email	35
30 mail	29 burn	28	27 finish	26 jump
21	22 invite	23 arrive	24 rain	25 mix
20 clean	19 glue	18 brush	17 paint	16
11 shop	12	13 study	14 score	15 race
10 drop	9 sled	8 text	7 open	6 start
1 play	2 smile	3	4 visit	5 kick

63

7 Dress sense

🔦 **Show what you know!** What clothes words can you remember?

Listening 1 🎧 Listen and check (✓) the clothes words you hear.

2 🎧 Listen again. Say "yes" or "no."

1 Alex might wear jeans to the disco. — Yes.
2 Dan thinks he may look better with a coat.
3 It isn't cold. Alex might not wear a jacket.
4 Dan feels like a rock star.
5 Alex looks like Mr. Parker.
6 Maria thinks they should write about pop music.

3 Read and order the words.

1 might / a / Dan / shirt. / wear / striped
2 jacket? / wear / Who / a / might
3 not / wear / I / a sweater / tonight. / might
4 hot / may / a coat. / be too / It / to wear
5 a shirt. / Alex / wear / might
6 lot in / They / the disco. / might / dance a

🔍 **LOOK**

I think it **may** look better with a jacket.
You **might** feel like a rock star.
I **might not** wear a jacket.

4 Look at the pictures. Read and match.

> a I'm sorry, Peter. We may not have time. I have a lot to do this afternoon.
> b I don't know. It's cold. I might wear my coat or I might wear my jacket.
> c I think I might, or I may wear a skirt.
> d She says she might come, but she needs to finish her homework first.

1 What are you going to wear to watch the soccer game?

2 Are you going to wear your pants to the disco?

3 Is Mary going to come to the disco on Friday?

4 Can we go to the park on our way home, please?

5 Practice the conversations with your friend. Write another conversation together.

6 Write questions with "might."
1 When / go / disco?
   When might you go to the disco?
2 What clothes / wear / disco?
3 What music / dance to / disco?
4 Who / take / pictures of?
5 Who / go with?
6 What / take / with you?

7 Ask and answer.

> When might you go to the disco?

> I think I might go next week.

8 Play the game. What's in the bag? Write sentences with "may."

It may be a scarf.

Reading 9 Read and find two things that people used differently a long time ago.

http://www.cambridge.org/elt/kidsbox/ezine

Kid's Box Ezine!

home | reports | games | world | email

★ Fashions may come and go, but some fashion extras haven't changed for centuries.

Kid's Box reports Fashion

Buttons hold clothes together and decorate them. Today buttons are made of plastic, metal, glass, and shells, but the ancient Greeks had buttons made of gold.

Men and women have worn belts for about 5,000 years. People first used them to carry things, then, much later, to hold their pants up.

Did you know that the first umbrellas protected people from the Sun? Now there are big golf umbrellas and small, light umbrellas that we can carry in a purse.

Your grandfather probably wore shorts to school when he was 14! These days we usually wear them for sports and when it's very hot.

The first pockets were small bags that people wore on their belts. Thieves could take them easily, so people put the bags inside their clothes. Then it was difficult to get money out, so in the 18th century people sewed pockets into their clothes.

Women and girls wear stockings under their skirts and dresses to cover their legs in cold weather. Stockings can be light and thin or thick and heavy. They are usually made of nylon or wool.

People usually wear gloves on their hands when it's cold, but some people use gloves at work, for example, firefighters.

button | umbrella | gloves | pocket | belt | stockings | decorate | shorts

10 Listen. Repeat the word. Do you wear it? Say "yes" or "no."   ▶ 1 Belt.   Belt. Yes.

11 Read again and complete.

bags   Sun   Stockings   shorts   Gloves   ~~buttons~~

1 The ancient Greeks had gold _buttons_ .
2 The first umbrellas protected people from the _____ .
3 _____ protect our hands.
4 The first pockets were small _____ .
5 Older boys wore _____ to school 60 years ago.
6 _____ are usually made of nylon or wool.

66

12 Read and match.

1. It's very hot today.
2. My pants are falling down.
3. Look at those black clouds.
4. I can't find my money.
5. Hey, I like your striped stockings!
6. The cook has really big gloves.

a. They stop her burning her hands.
b. He's wearing a T-shirt and shorts.
c. They look great with that skirt.
d. I need a belt!
e. It isn't in my pocket!
f. I might take my umbrella.

13 Read and say the words.

There's a great new dance, and we do it in school.
School disco! School disco!

Turn to the ⬅ .

Turn to the ➡ .

Turn around and around.

Dance ⬆ and ⬇ .

School disco!

Long striped 👗 ,

Big spotted 👕 ,

🎩 and 🧥 ,

And beautiful 👗 .

🧦 and 🧣 ,

🔘 and 💍 ,

Walking out
Like queens and kings.
School disco!

Big square 👔 ,

〰 and 🧤 ,

👖 and 🧥 –

The clothes that we love.

Chorus

School disco!

14 🔊 Listen and check. Sing the song.

15 Play the game. Who is it?

"He's wearing gray shorts."

"It might be "i.""

"No! He's wearing …"

16 **Focus on phonics**

When I'm sad, I say …
When I'm tired, I say …
When I'm angry, I say …
When I'm surprised, I say …
When I'm happy, I say …
And when I'm excited, I say …

umbrella

Speaking **17** Find ten differences with your friend.

In picture a, there's …

Writing **18** Write about one of the pictures.

In picture a, there are some people outside a movie theater. I can see …

Joke Corner

What's the last thing you take off before you go to bed?

You take your feet off the floor!

History | Clothes

FACT: The first "tattoos" came from the Pacific island of Tahiti.

1 Read and find the clothes that come from places a–d on the map.

Today clothes are made in factories, but many years ago people made clothes by hand with natural materials.

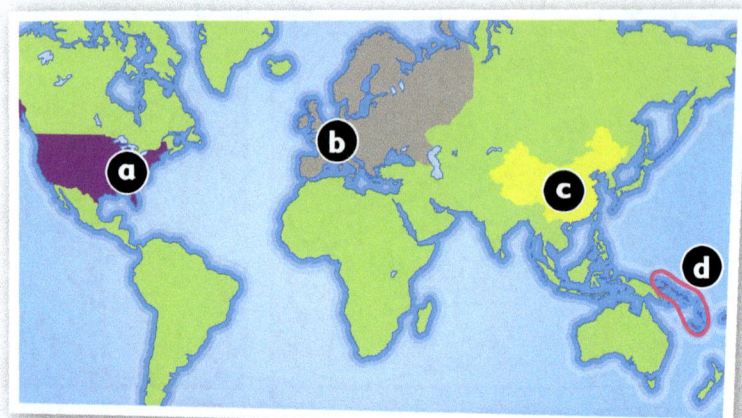

On the Pacific islands, people made their first clothes from leaves and from bark, which is on the outside of a tree. For dancing, men and women wore skirts made of grass and a headdress of flowers, feathers, and shells. They also had earrings made of bones and shells.

Most Native North American men wore a long rectangular piece of leather with a belt, sometimes with leather pants when it was cold. Leather is made from cow skin. Others wore pants made of fur. Most men didn't wear shirts. The women wore skirts, pants, or dresses made from cloth or leather. Both men and women wore leather shoes. These are called moccasins.

People in China started to wear Han clothes more than 3,000 years ago. They are made of silk, a cloth that comes from the silkworm. Some people still wear Han clothes today: a shirt, a jacket, a skirt or pants, and white socks and black shoes made of cotton.

In Europe 2,000 years ago, men wore tunics. This is like a long T-shirt that comes down to your knees or your feet. When it was cold, they wore shirts under their tunics, and some men wore stockings or pants. It was only 500 years ago when men stopped wearing stockings.

2 Find these words.
1. the outside part of a tree
2. something for your head
3. special Native American shoes
4. special clothes from China
5. the hair of animals
6. rings for your ears

3 🎧 Listen and answer.

4 Read and match.

A lot of people have to wear special clothes at work or in school. These are called uniforms.

This is William. He's a firefighter in California, U.S.A. In this picture he's wearing his day uniform. This is a shirt, which is made of cotton, and special pants. He wears his day uniform when he isn't fighting fires.

a

b

c

d

e

f

g  [1]

1 Strong boots protect his feet. They are made of rubber and metal.

2 He wears these pants over his day uniform. They're big, so he can jump into them quickly. They have strong cloth over the knees to protect them and a plastic stripe at the bottom above the feet, so people can see him in the dark.

3 His jacket protects the top of his body and helps him to stay dry. There are big pockets to carry things like a radio and his gloves.

4 He wears a special scarf around his neck that he can pull up over his head to protect it.

5 His mask is very important. It protects his face and eyes from the fire. It also protects his lungs because he must not breathe in gases.

6 His helmet is made of leather. Firefighters' helmets today are almost the same as the first ones from more than 150 years ago, but they're better and stronger.

7 The last things the firefighter puts on are his gloves. These are made of leather, and they protect his hands from the fire.

Project

Design and write about a uniform.

You need:
- Paper
- Colors

How to design the uniform:
1 Choose a job (a real one or one that you imagine).
2 Draw, label, and color the picture.
3 Write about the different parts of the uniform.
4 Make a class book.

8 Around the world

🔦 **Show what you know!** What countries can you remember?

Listening ① 🎧 02 CD4 Listen and check (✓) the countries you hear.

② 🎧 03 CD4 Listen again. Who said it?

1 I've already found four.
2 Have you written the article on Mexico yet?
3 I've just cleaned my desk.
4 I haven't saved the article yet.
5 They've just given the names of the competition winners.
6 You've just cleaned them up.

③ Read and match.

1 Have you spoken to
2 I've just spent
3 I haven't met
4 I've just found out some really
5 Frank's already
6 She's just sent an email

a interesting things about India.
b the new French teacher yet.
c left school.
d ten dollars on a new T-shirt.
e to her sister in Japan.
f your mom about the field trip yet?

🔍 **LOOK**

Have you written the article on Mexico **yet**?
I haven't saved the article **yet**.
I've **already** found four.
I've **just** cleaned my desk.

4 Read and complete.

| been | packed | cleaned | done |
| begun | played | bought | put |

We've just finished school, our vacation's (1) **begun**.
We've (2) _____ our last exam, now we're, we're going to have fun.
We've just (3) _____ away our books, and we've (4) _____ our desks.
So we're all going home. It's time to have a rest!

Yes, it's vacation time! Time to have a break.
Yes, it's vacation time, and we're all feeling great.

We've (5) _____ in the park, and we've (6) _____ to the zoo.
We've already (7) _____ some summer clothes, too.
But we haven't (8) _____ our suitcase, and we're going to go away
To swim in the ocean and sleep and play all day.

Chorus
… Yes, it's vacation time …

5 Listen and check. Sing the song.

6 Read and choose the right words.

Hi, Sarah,
How are you? I've been in Australia **(1)** just / for / already a week now, but I **(2)** since / yet / still haven't seen a koala!
We've **(3)** ever / just / for left Sydney, and we're driving to the beach. Have you **(4)** since / already / ever seen a picture of Sydney Harbour Bridge or Sydney Opera House? They're amazing. I've **(5)** already / yet / never taken a hundred pictures, and we haven't been to the famous coral reef **(6)** ever / yet / for. We'll visit it tomorrow. I can't wait!
I haven't heard from you **(7)** never / just / since we arrived.
You must tell me your news!
Love,
Emma

7 Write the sentences. Put the words in the correct place.

1 (already) I've eaten breakfast.
   I've already eaten breakfast.
2 (yet) I haven't done my homework.
3 (yet) Have you spoken to your teacher?
4 (just) We've been to the museum.
5 (already) They've written the article.
6 (just) He's gone to school.

8 Guess and write an answer for each sentence. Ask and answer. How many of your guesses were right?

1 Something that you've done, but no one else in the class has done yet.
2 Something that about half the class has never done, but want to do.
3 Something that about half the class has done since they got up.
4 A free-time activity that half the class has done for more than three years.

Reading

9 Read and think. How many of these countries aren't in Europe?

http://www.cambridge.org/elt/kidsbox/ezine

Kid's Box Ezine!

home | reports | games | world | email

Kid's Box reports — Countries

Well, this is our last ezine this year. We've won the prize to write for the international ezine, so today we're going to tell you about some of the other countries in the competition.

In India they speak more than 24 languages, but Hindi and English are the two most important languages. Indians love movies, and in a year, more movies are made in Bollywood than in Hollywood in the U.S.A.

Mexico is in North America, but the Mexicans have spoken Spanish there for hundreds of years. More people speak Spanish in Mexico than in Spain. Did you know that modern chewing gum first came from trees in Mexico in the 19th century?

More tourists visit France than any other country: about 83 million every year. The French also have the most famous bike race in the world, which is called the Tour de France.

Brazil is the fifth-biggest country in the world. The people from Brazil are Brazilian, but they speak Portuguese. Besides Portugal and Brazil, people speak Portuguese in five other countries.

Germany has the biggest population in Europe. About 81 million people live there. The Germans make more cars than any other European country. The famous composers Bach, Beethoven, and Wagner were all German, too.

Greece is not an island, but there are about 2,000 Greek islands. A lot of the words we use today, like "mathematics" and "telephone," come from Greek.

Brazil | India | France | Mexico | Germany | Portugal | Greece | Spain

Brazilian | Indian | French | Mexican | German | Portuguese | Greek | Spanish

10 Listen. Repeat the country and say the nationality. ▶ 1 Greece.

Greece. Greek.

11 Read again and answer.

1 Where did chewing gum come from?
2 Which country gets the most visitors?
3 Name the world's fifth-biggest country.
4 Where was Bach from?
5 What happens in Bollywood?
6 Which old language gives us modern words?

12   Listen and check (✓) the countries you hear.

India		
Mexico		
Italy		
France		
Brazil		
Germany	✓	Berlin
Greece		
Spain		
U.S.A.		
Portugal		

13   Listen again and write the capital cities.

14 Look and answer.

1 What is the capital of Spain?
2 Which capital here is the closest to Rome?
3 Which capital here is the farthest south?
4 Which country is Lisbon the capital of?
5 Which capital here is the farthest east?
6 How many capitals here are north of Paris?

15 Read and correct the sentences.

Archie Mendes is the smartest boy in Europe. His mother's Greek, but his father's Portuguese, so he speaks both of these languages perfectly. He also speaks English, which he's spoken since he was three, and French.

He's only 12 years old, but he's studied at the Sorbonne University in Paris for two years. He's just helped some engineers design an amazing new car that goes on land and on water.

He loves traveling, and he's already been to India and Mexico, but he hasn't been to Brazil yet. He's had an invitation to visit a friend, so he's going to go there for his summer vacation.

He's just come back from Bollywood, where he helped make a new movie. He likes doing a lot of different things in his free time, but his favorite hobby is free running. He's just made a short video. In it, we can see him running through streets and jumping from wall to wall beautifully. He knows he always has to wear special clothes to protect his body when he does this. That's what makes him the smartest boy in Europe!

1 Archie's parents are German and Portuguese.
2 Archie speaks Greek, Portuguese, Spanish, and French.
3 He's spoken English since he was five.
4 He's studied in the capital of Spain for two years.
5 He's just helped some engineers design an amazing new boat that goes on land and on water.
6 He's already been to India, but he hasn't been to Mexico yet.
7 He's only 12, but he's already helped to make a car and a TV show.
8 He's just made a short video on long jumping.

16 Focus on phonics

What languages do you speak?
German, French, Spanish, and Greek.

And which cities do you call home?
Berlin, Paris, Madrid, and Rome.

Speaking 17 Ask and answer. Find your partner.

- How long has she been here?
- She's been here for five minutes.

Writing 18 Answer the questions. Write about what you've done this year and in Unit 8.

1 Have you learned to use the past in English?
2 Have you finished this book yet?
3 Have you taken any exams yet?
4 Have you just learned about countries?
5 You still haven't read the story, have you?
6 Have you done your project yet?

This year I've ..., but I haven't ...
In Unit 8 I've ..., but I haven't ...

Joke Corner

What is in the middle of Paris, America, and Australia?

The letter "r"!

Language: The history of words

FACT: English is the only language that uses a capital letter for the word "I."

1 Read and answer.

1. How many English words have you studied?
2. Where does the word "England" come from?

If you've studied all seven *Kid's Box* books, you've learned more than 1,140 words, and you've seen more than 200 verbs. That's a lot of English words! But where do these words all come from?

Like many languages, English uses words from other languages. This started a long time ago when the Romans invaded England. Then it continued when different German tribes, the Angles, Saxons, and Jutes, arrived. Some of the words they brought are "kitchen," "pepper," and "cheese." The name "England" also comes from these "Angles," and the country was then called "Englaland." The people spoke a language that we now call "Old English." This is similar to the language of the Vikings, who invaded later. Viking words include "egg," "leg," "sky," and "window."

In 1066, the Normans from France invaded England, and English changed a lot.

During the next 300 years, the kings and queens liked speaking French, so English took a lot of words from French, for example, "art," "mirror," and "dance." Since the Normans, no one has invaded England.

Words like "pajamas" and "shampoo" came from India in the 19th century, but English didn't take many more new words from other languages until people started to travel more in the 20th century. English now uses many food words from different countries, for example, "pizza" and "pasta" from Italian and "frankfurter" from German.

What do you think?

There are also a lot of international sports words, for example the Japanese sports "karate" and "judo." Are they the same in your language? Did they come from English or from the countries where people first played the sport?

2 Listen and find the words.

3 Read and label the pictures.

> telescope   ~~telephone~~
> microphone   television

"Tele-" is a prefix. That means we can put it in front of a word and it changes the meaning of the word. It means "far" and comes from ancient Greek. We can put "-phone" at the end of a word to change the meaning. It is a suffix. It means "sound."

1 _telephone_   2 _____

3 _____   4 _____

4 Complete the chart. Answer the questions.

Prefixes	Root words
	market, graph, scope, hero, cycle, angle, copy, star, ground, chip
bi-	*bicycle*
super-	
tri-	
micro-	
photo-	
mega-	
under-	

1 What do the new words in the chart mean?
2 "Un-" is another prefix. Can you think of any words that start with "un-"? How does it change the word?

Project
Make a poster about your language.

You need:
- The Internet or encyclopedias
- Newspapers and magazines to cut words out of

How to make the poster:
1 Find out about your language on the Internet or in encyclopedias. Answer these questions:
- When did people start to speak it?
- How many people speak it?
- Do they speak it in any other countries?
- Which words has it taken from other languages? Where are they from?
2 Write about your language.
3 Draw a map of your country showing people bringing new words.
4 What English words are there in your language?

Review Units  and

1 William is talking to his friend, Sarah. What does Sarah say? Read the conversation and choose the best answer. Write a letter (A–H) for your answer.

	William:	Hi, Sarah. How are you?
	Sarah:	B _____
	William:	What are you writing in your notebook?
1	**Sarah:**	_____ .
	William:	When are you going to Mexico?
2	**Sarah:**	_____ .
	William:	What's the weather like in Mexico?
3	**Sarah:**	_____ .
	William:	They speak Spanish in Mexico. Do you speak Spanish?
4	**Sarah:**	_____ .
	William:	Have you been to Mexico before?
5	**Sarah:**	_____ .
	William:	You're so lucky!

A Not yet. I went to Mexico last week.
B I'm fine, thanks.
C Never. This is the first time.
D Tomorrow afternoon. I need to get ready today.
E Very much. It's sunny most days.
F It's a list of all the things I need to take on vacation. I haven't packed my suitcase yet.
G It might be hot. So I'll have to take lots of T-shirts and shorts.
H A little. I want to learn more when I'm there.

2   Listen and draw lines. There is one example.

David   Emma   Harry   Katy   Betty   Michael   Helen

80

3 Play the game. Ask and answer.

Guess the country

Instructions
- Roll a die and move around the board.
- Answer your friends' questions.
- If you make a mistake, miss a turn.

Where's he from? — He's from the U.S.A.
What nationality is she? — She's Colombian.
Where's this from? — It's from Italy.

Values
Units 1 & 2

Living with technology

1 Read and choose "yes" or "no." Are you A, B, or C?

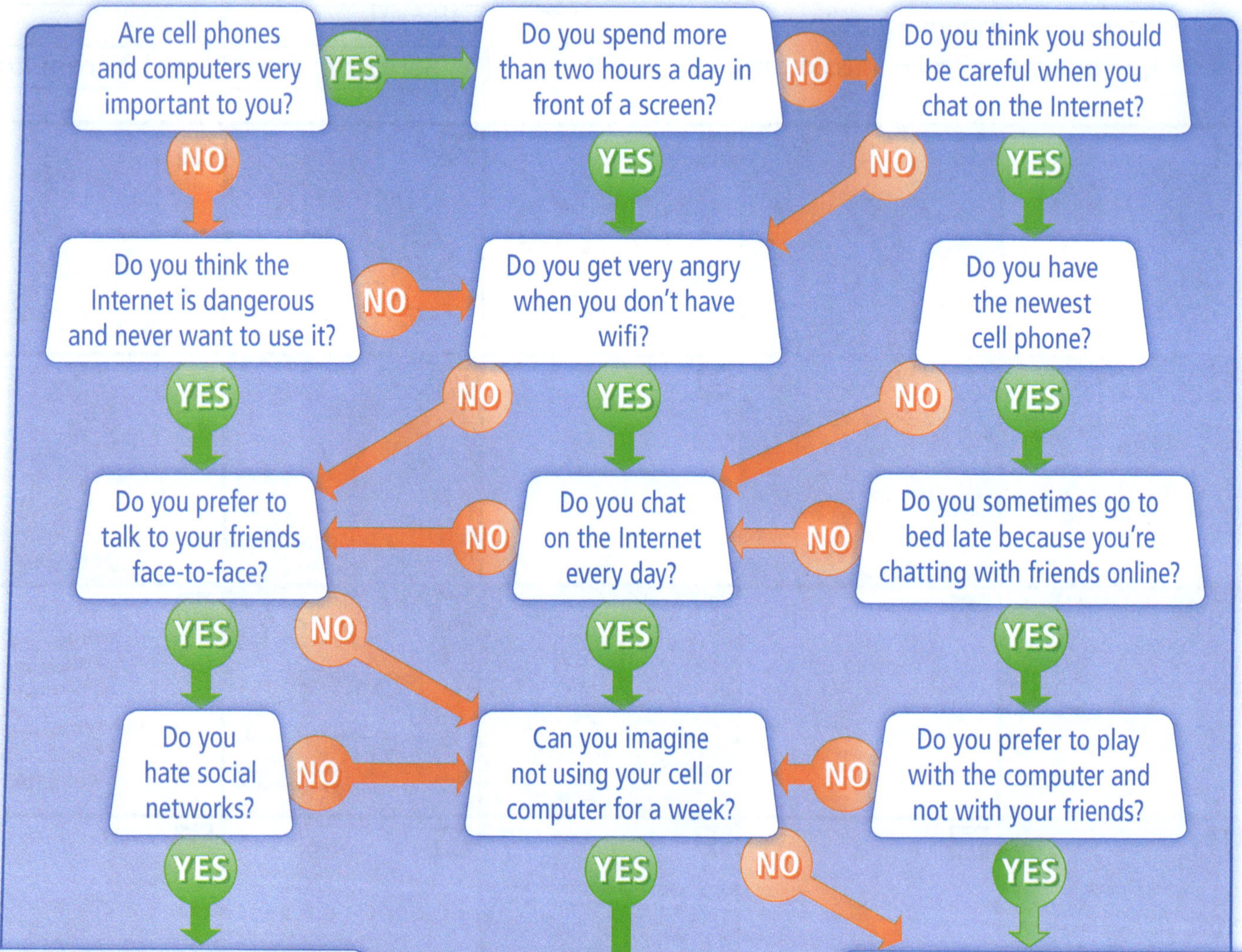

- Are cell phones and computers very important to you?
  - YES → Do you spend more than two hours a day in front of a screen?
    - NO → Do you think you should be careful when you chat on the Internet?
  - NO → Do you think the Internet is dangerous and never want to use it?

- Do you get very angry when you don't have wifi?
- Do you have the newest cell phone?
- Do you prefer to talk to your friends face-to-face?
- Do you chat on the Internet every day?
- Do you sometimes go to bed late because you're chatting with friends online?
- Do you hate social networks?
- Can you imagine not using your cell or computer for a week?
- Do you prefer to play with the computer and not with your friends?

A   Internet-free
It's good that you like meeting your friends and seeing them face-to-face, but remember that technology is an important part of everyday life. You should try to use it more now because it'll be the communication of the future.

B   A good mix
You enjoy chatting to your friends on the Internet, but you also like going out and meeting them in person. You know how to make good use of technology and have time for your friends.

C   Be careful
You spend a lot of time with computers and cell phones, but you shouldn't forget your friends. You should try to meet them more often. Remember that talking to people face-to-face is also great fun.

2 Do you agree with your result for Activity 1? Talk to your friend. Ask and answer.

1. How many hours a day do you spend in front of a screen?
2. Do you think one hour a day is too much or not enough?
3. How many hours a week do you spend with your friends?
4. What are the problems if you spend too much time in front of a screen?

Be safe at home

Values — Units 3 & 4

1 Look at the picture. What's wrong? Talk to your friend.

- Look at "a." What do you think is wrong?
- His hands are dirty.
- Yes. We should wash our hands before we eat.

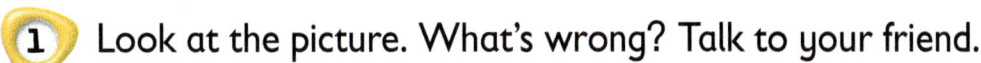

2 Listen and check your ideas. Say the letter a–h.

3 Ask and answer.

1. Why should we be careful with hot things?
2. Why is a wet floor dangerous?
3. Should we stand on chairs to get things from a high shelf?
4. What's the problem if we don't wash our hands before we eat?
5. Why should we sit on our chairs correctly?
6. What other dangerous places are there in a house?

Values
Units 5 & 6

Harmony at home

1 Read and answer the questions.
1. Why is Mr. Banks often away from home?
2. How does the family work as a team?
3. What have Fred and Vicky learned?

http://www.davidsreports.co.uk

David's reports

This week I've been to visit the Banks family. They all help do the jobs around the house and take care of Mrs. Banks.

David Well, Mr. Banks, can you tell us about your family and how you all work together?

Mr. Banks Yes, of course. My son Fred's 16, and my daughter Vicky's 13. We've worked hard as a family this year because my wife has been very sick.

David Oh, I'm sorry. What do you mean when you say "worked hard"?

Mr. Banks Well, during the year I've often been away from home. I take my wife to the hospital, and I spend a lot of time there. So Fred and Vicky have learned to do a lot of things: they sometimes do the shopping, and when Fred cooks our meals, Vicky cleans the kitchen.

David Not many children know how to cook and clean!

Mr. Banks No. Fred saw the problem and asked me how he could help at home. We spent some Saturdays in the kitchen, and I showed him how to make good meals. Now he's an excellent cook! Actually, he likes to choose the food himself so he prefers to do the shopping.

David That's great! And did you say that Vicky helps him in the kitchen?

Mr. Banks That's right. She helps in a lot of other ways, too. Vicky cleans the house and does the laundry.

David That's great, Vicky! How do you feel about doing all these jobs?

Vicky Well, actually, I don't see it as extra work now. It was difficult at first because I felt that I didn't have enough time to do these jobs, do my homework, and meet my friends. Now I've learned to do things better and faster, so I have a little more time. We all work as a team, and I feel good because I'm part of it. I'm very lucky to have a brother like Fred. He's been great.

David That's a nice thing to hear your sister say. How do you feel about that, Fred?

Fred Yes, it is a very nice thing to say, and I feel good, thanks. I think that before all this, I was actually a little lazy. I didn't do anything in the house, and my parents had to do everything. Now I'm really happy that I've learned to do a lot of things for myself and for others. I think we're both happy to help our parents. The most important thing for us is that Mom is feeling better now.

2 Listen and say "Vicky," "Fred," or "Mr. Banks."

Sharing problems

Values — Units 7 & 8

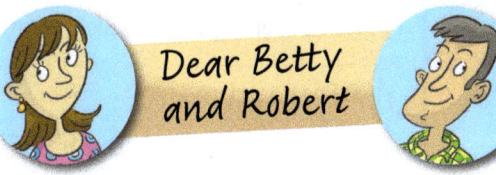

1 Read the letters and answer the questions.

Dear Betty and Robert,

Last week I found my 11-year-old sister, Kim, crying in her bedroom. She told me that some other children at school have sent her horrible messages on her cell phone. She said this isn't the first time it's happened and that she's been unhappy about it for three weeks. She says the children who are doing it think it's funny and that it's only a joke, but she's very worried, so she doesn't want to go to school. She's asked me not to tell my parents. What should I do?

Yours,

Maggie (14 years old)

1 Why was Kim crying?
2 How long has she been unhappy?
3 Do you think it's funny?

Dear Maggie,

This is very serious. Your sister is very unhappy. If she doesn't want to go to school, she needs help right now. This situation has lasted long enough, and it might get worse. You've listened to your sister, and this has helped her, but she really needs the advice of a grown-up. You must tell your parents. It might be a good idea for them to speak to your sister's teachers. We can understand that you may feel that you shouldn't tell your parents the secret, but it's really the best way to help your sister.

Yours,

Betty and Robert

4 What does Kim need?
5 What must Maggie do?

Dear Betty and Robert,

An old friend has moved into the house next to mine. We've been friends since we were three, but she's a girl. She's very funny, and she makes me laugh, but my friends on the basketball team have started to call me horrible names because I'm friends with a girl. They've blocked me, so I can't chat with them on the Internet. I feel very angry and unhappy, but I don't want to lose any of my friends. Please help me. What should I do?

Yours,

Jim

6 What's the problem with Jim's old friend?
7 Why does Jim feel angry and unhappy?

2 Talk to your friend about Jim's letter. Imagine that you are Betty and Robert.

1 Who can Jim talk to?
2 What should Jim do?

3 Write a reply to Jim's letter. Use the language in the box.

| might | should / shouldn't | need to | must / must not |

Grammar reference

Going to
We use *going to* to talk about plans.

Affirmative	Negative (n't = not)	Question
I'm going to catch the bus.	I'm not going to catch the bus.	Am I going to catch the bus?
She's going to catch the bus.	She isn't going to catch the bus.	Is she going to catch the bus?
They're going to catch the bus.	They aren't going to catch the bus.	Are they going to catch the bus?

Will
We use *will* to talk about the future.

Affirmative	Negative (n't = not)	Question
It'll travel to the Moon.	It won't travel to the Moon.	Will it travel to the Moon?
We'll travel to the Moon.	We won't travel to the Moon.	Will we travel to the Moon?

Past progressive
We use the *past progressive* to describe what was happening in the past.

Affirmative	Negative (n't = not)	Question
I was working when you arrived.	I wasn't working when you arrived.	Was I working when you arrived?
He was working when you arrived.	He wasn't working when you arrived.	Was he working when you arrived?
They were working when you arrived.	They weren't working when you arrived.	Were they working when you arrived?

Count and non-count nouns

Count nouns	Non-count nouns
We can count them: apples, bananas, carrots	We can't count them: bread, sugar, water
How many bananas are there?	How much water is there?
There are too many bananas.	There's too much water.
There aren't many bananas.	There isn't much water.
There aren't enough bananas.	There isn't enough water.

5. Present perfect and adverbs

I still haven't done my homework. (= But I have to do it soon.)

She's been sick since Monday. (= When? A point in time: time, date, day, etc.)
They've been sick for two days. (= How long? How many minutes, hours, days, weeks, etc.)

Have you ever had a fish for a pet? (= At any time in your life)
I've never seen a dolphin. (= Not at any time in my life)

6. Quantifiers

some someone something somewhere	any anyone anything anywhere	no no one nothing nowhere	every everyone everything everywhere
There's someone at the door.	There isn't anyone at the door. Is there anyone at the door?	There's no one at the door.	Everyone's at the door.
I have something to tell you.	I don't have anything to tell you. Do you have anything to tell me?	I have nothing to tell you.	I'm going to tell you everything.
They're going somewhere.	They aren't going anywhere. Are they going anywhere?	They're going nowhere.	They're going everywhere.

7. Possibility

I may buy the skirt.   I may not buy the skirt.
It might rain.   It might not rain.

8. Present perfect and adverbs

You've just sent the email.	You haven't sent the email yet.	Have you sent the email yet?
She's already sent the email.	She hasn't sent the email yet.	Has she sent the email yet?

Flyers practice test

Listening

Part 1 5 questions

 Listen and draw lines. There is one example.

Katy   Harry   Helen   William

Sue   Jack   Emma

Part 2 5 questions

 Listen and write. There is one example.

The music teacher

1 **Teaches:** the _____guitar_____
2 **Name:** Betty _____
3 **Address:** 45 _____ Street
4 **No lessons:** weekends or _____
5 **Lesson times:** after _____
6 **Phone number:** _____

Part 3 5 questions

19 CD4 Where did the baby put these things? Listen and write a letter in each box. There is one example.

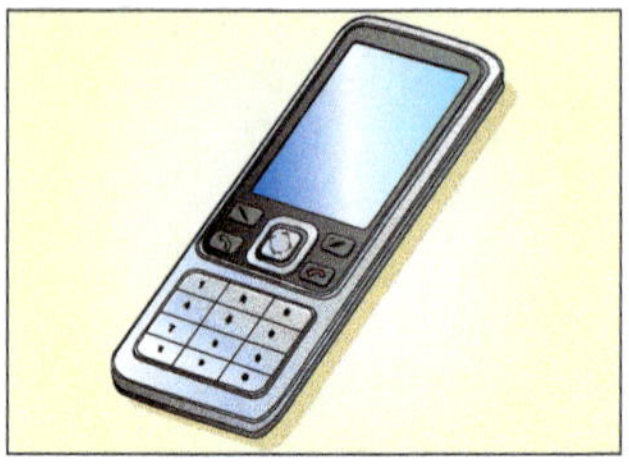

cell phone C

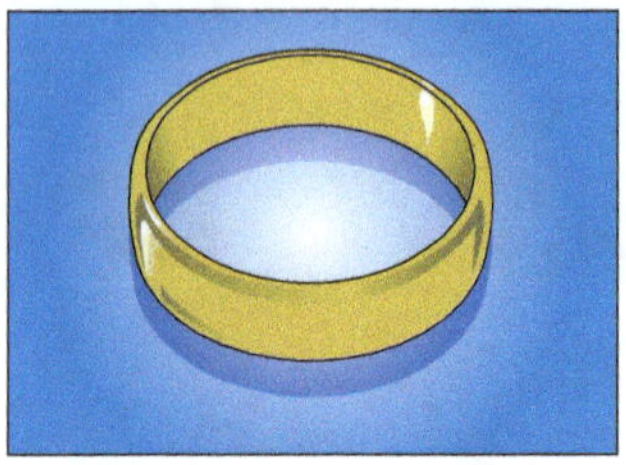

ring ☐

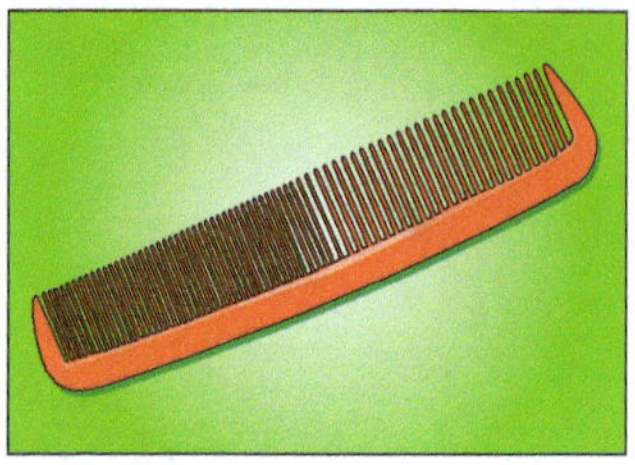

comb ☐

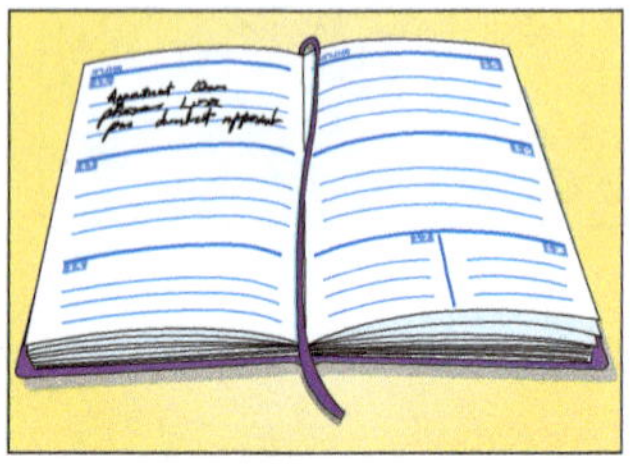

diary ☐

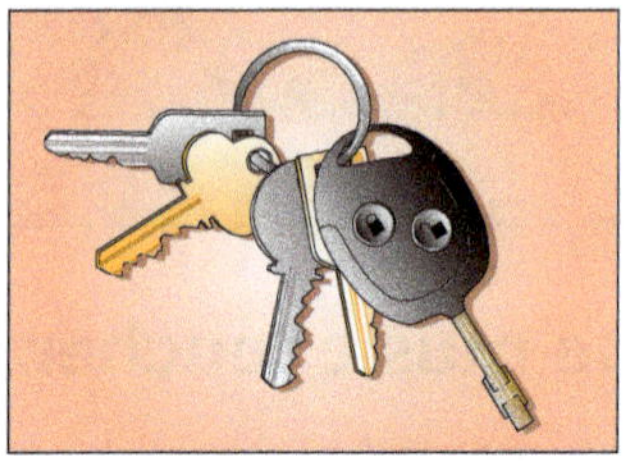

keys ☐

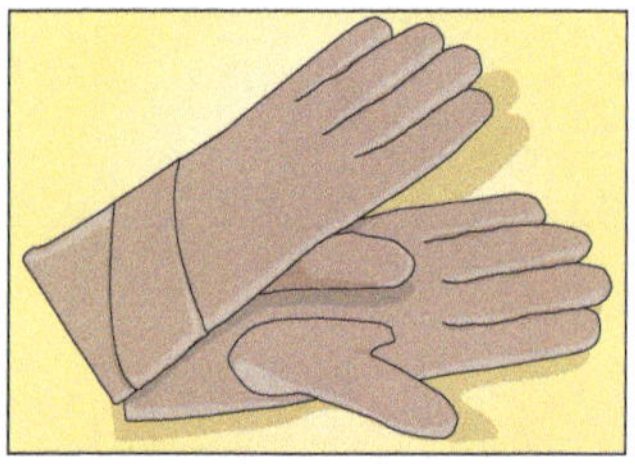

gloves ☐

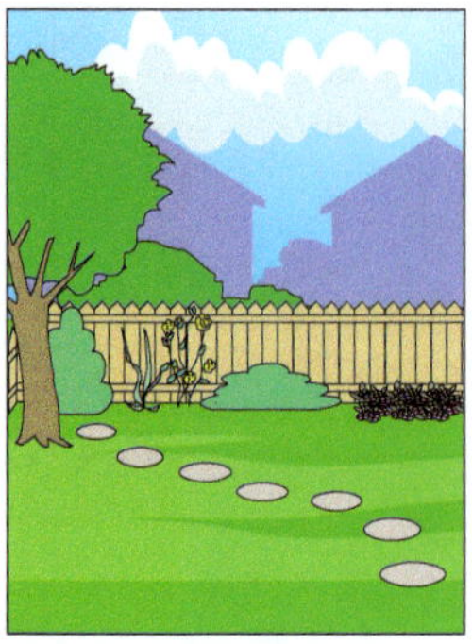

A

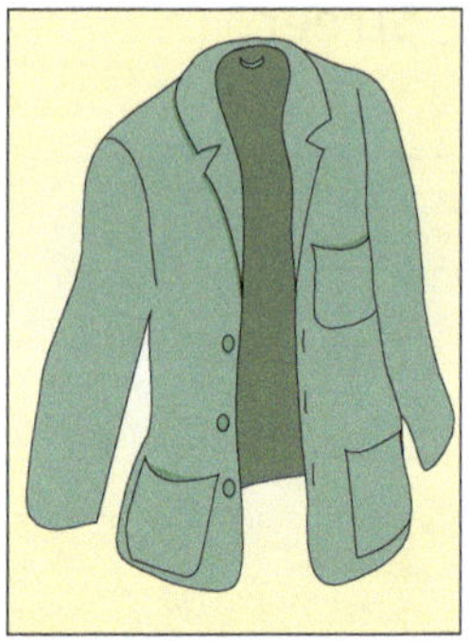

B

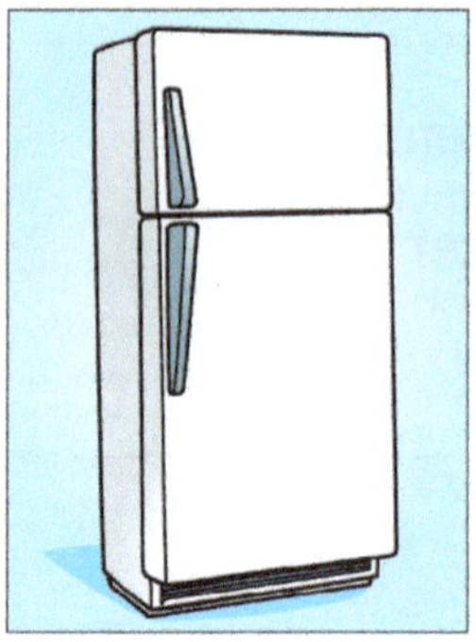

C

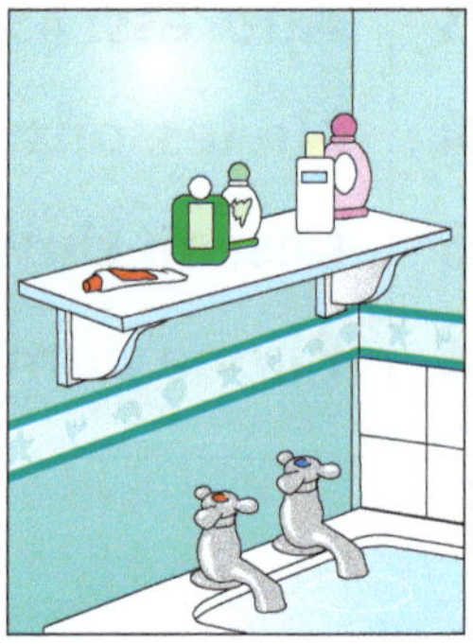

D

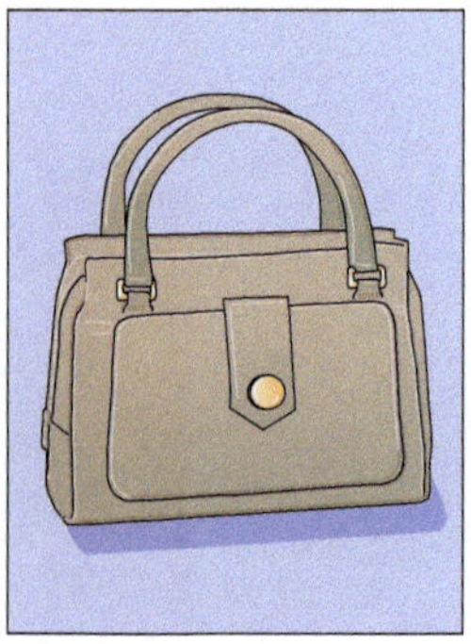

E

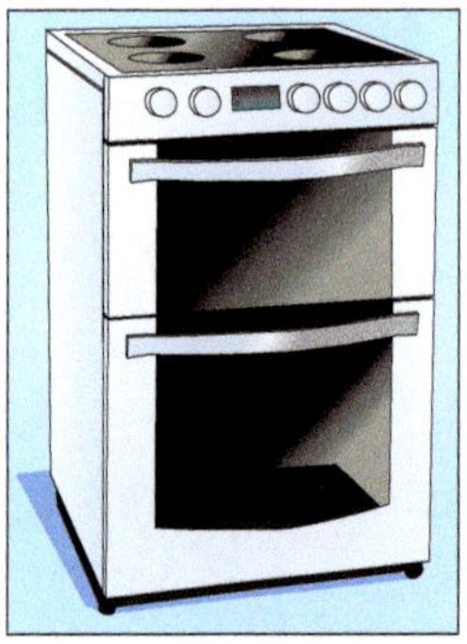

F

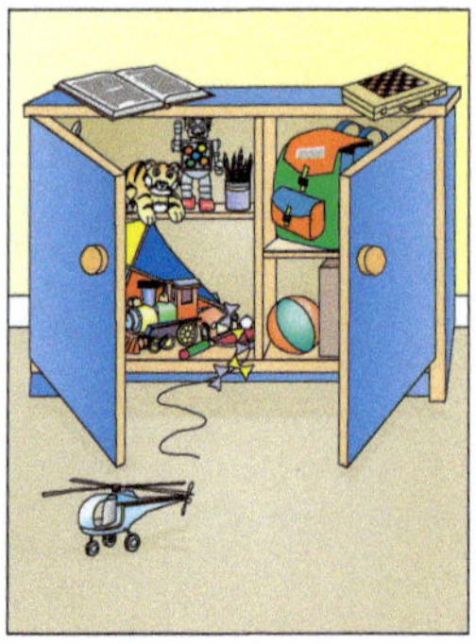

G

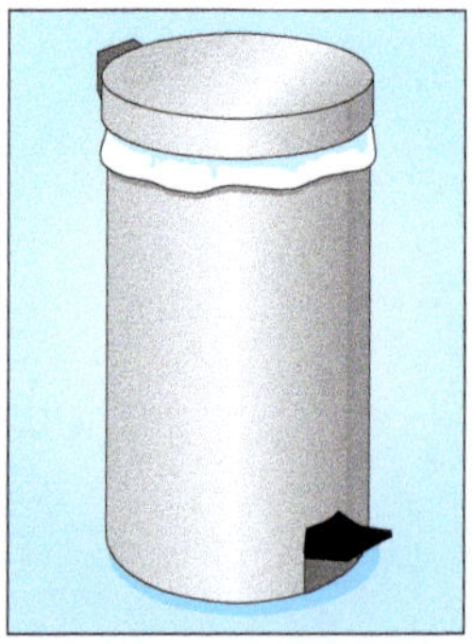

H

Part 4 5 questions

 Listen and check (✓) the box. There is one example.

How will Fred help his mom?

A ☐

B ✓

C ☐

1 What will they have for lunch?

A ☐

B ☐

C ☐

2 What does Mary look like?

A ☐

B ☐

C ☐

91

3 What time will Mary's train arrive?

A ☐

B ☐

C ☐

4 What's Mary's job?

A ☐

B ☐

C ☐

5 What will they all do together?

A ☐

B ☐

C ☐

Part 5   5 questions

Listen and color and write. There is one example.

Flyers practice test — Reading & Writing

Part **1** 10 questions

Look and read. Choose the correct words and write them on the lines. There is one example.

astronauts

a university

an octopus

a fire station

a kangaroo

a puppy

We see actors on TV, in movies and sometimes in this place.	a theater
1 You go to this place to buy stamps and to post letters and postcards.	....
2 This animal lives in the ocean and it has eight legs.	....
3 In this place you can sometimes see extinct animals.	....
4 These people can help you when you have a toothache.	....
5 When this young animal grows older, it is called a dog.	....
6 These people have to be very brave because they go into space in rockets.	....
7 You can study different subjects, like math and geography, in this place.	....
8 These people work in the kitchens of places like restaurants and hospitals.	....
9 This small green animal is very good at jumping.	....
10 If someone steals something from you, you should go to this place.	....

a frog

cooks

~~a theater~~

a whale

a hotel

a museum

a post office   a police station   dentists

Part 2   5 questions

Helen is talking to Sarah, a singer who is visiting her school.
What does Sarah say?

Read the conversation and choose the best answer.
Write a letter (A–H) for each answer.

You do not need to use all the letters.

Example

Helen: When did you start singing?

Sarah: _____ B _____

Questions

1 **Helen:** Do you write the songs that you sing?

   Sarah: _____

2 **Helen:** How many songs have you written?

   Sarah: _____

3 **Helen:** Have you done any other jobs?

   Sarah: _____

4 **Helen:** Do you enjoy being a singer?

   Sarah: _____

5 **Helen:** Please will you sing something for us?

   Sarah: _____

A I don't know. Hundreds!

B I can't remember. I was very young! **(Example)**

C I love it! It's the best job in the world.

D Usually, but not always.

E It's hard to write good songs.

F Of course. What song would you like to hear?

G Yes, they can.

H Once I worked in a café.

Part 3   6 questions

Read the story. Choose a word from the box.
Write the correct word next to numbers 1–5. There is one example.

Example

| ~~weekend~~ | heavy | sounded | wet | backpack |
| whispered | smart | feel | tent | office |

It was my birthday last _____weekend_____ and Dad took me to a circus. I love

seeing animals and people who do **(1)** _____ things. We saw some horses that

jumped over boxes and danced, and a beautiful girl on a very high swing.

The circus was in a big **(2)** _____ and after an hour it got hot.

"I have a headache," I **(3)** _____ to Dad. "Can we go?"

"Just wait a minute," he said. "The clowns are coming now and they're your favorites."

Then two clowns ran in. One of them pointed at me and said,

"I need a child to help me. Come on!"

97

He gave me some water and we threw it at the other clown. We all got very

(4) _____ , but everyone laughed a lot.

When I sat down again, Dad said, "Do you (5) _____ OK now?"

"Yes," I said. "All that cold water made my headache better."

(6) Now choose the best name for the story.
Check one box.

Fun with the clowns ☐

A sad birthday ☐

A visit to the zoo ☐

Part 4   10 questions

Read the text. Choose the right words and write them on the lines.

Farms

Example | People who live in cities usually buy _____their_____ food in supermarkets,
1 | but most of _____ food comes from farms. At farms we can see plants and animals in the fields. Farmers get milk from cows and eggs from
2 | chickens, _____ they send to stores and markets. Sometimes
3 | _____ make butter and cheese from milk.

4 | In _____ hot countries, farmers can grow fruit, like oranges and lemons. In colder places, there are sheep farms. Sheep can live on high hills,
5 | _____ they eat grass. They give us wool for our clothes
6 | and meat _____ eat.

7 | Farmers have to work hard. They get _____ early in the morning
8 | and work outside all day. Plants _____ have water, so farmers like rain. When it's very hot, their fields get too dry. Sometimes lots of insects or animals, like rabbits, come and eat all the plants. Then the poor farmer
9 | _____ nothing to sell.

10 | Farmers also help to take _____ of the environment and all the beautiful flowers, birds, and butterflies that we enjoy when we visit the country.

Example	their	his	our
1	these	this	those
2	that	what	than
3	they	he	it
4	any	every	some
5	what	where	who
6	to	for	by
7	up	in	with
8	want	could	must
9	have	having	has
10	at	care	over

Part 5 7 questions

Look at the picture and read the story. Write some words to complete the sentences about the story. You can use 1, 2, 3, or 4 words.

The hungry snowman

My name is Anna. I live in a village in the mountains with my parents and my brother, Robert. Last Saturday it snowed, but on Sunday the sky was blue, and it was a beautiful day. Robert said, "Let's make a snowman!" We put on our coats and hats and ran into the yard. We made a very big snowball for the snowman's body and a smaller one for his head.

Then Robert said, "I'm going to get something." He went to the kitchen and brought a carrot for the snowman's nose and two potatoes for his eyes. Mom came outside to look at the snowman and said, "Would you like to stop work for a minute and have a snack?" She brought us hot drinks and some cookies. I said, "Let's finish the snowman first and eat the cookies later." We gave him an old scarf and arms made of wood from a tree.

Then my friend Vicky called me, and I went into the house and talked to her for a long time. When I came out again, I said, "We can eat the cookies now, Robert," but I couldn't find them. "Where are they?" I asked. "They've gone," he said. "The snowman ate them all." "That's strange," I said, "because the snowman doesn't have a mouth!"

Examples

Anna lives in _____a village_____ in the mountains.

_____Robert_____ is Anna's brother.

Questions

1 It snowed on _____, but Sunday was a beautiful day.

2 The children went into _____ to make a snowman.

3 The snowman's _____ was made from a large snowball.

4 Anna and Robert used _____ to give the snowman a nose.

5 Anna wanted to _____ first and eat the cookies later.

6 Anna talked to _____ for a long time.

7 The snowman couldn't eat because he didn't have _____!

Part 6 5 questions

Read the email and write the missing words. Write one word on each line.

Hello, Nick!

Example I have _____some_____ great news!

1 _____ you remember the afternoon in the summer vacation
2 that we spent in the park? We met our friends and _____
soccer with them. I took lots of pictures.

3 Well, I _____ one of the pictures to a magazine that had a
4 competition. Guess what? It won and it was a picture _____
you!

I won a very expensive new camera. I want to learn to take better pictures
5 with it, so Mom _____ going to find a teacher for me.

See you soon!

Alex

Part 7

Look at the three pictures. Write about this story. Write 20 or more words.